GW00725990

The Gestapo's Most Improbable Hostage

Author
Hugh Mallory Falconer
Squadron Leader 'Mallory'

(1910-1980)

The Gestapo's Most Improbable Hostage

By
Hugh Mallory Falconer
(SOE's Squadron Leader 'Mallory')

The story of a British officer who was
captured by the Gestapo while on a
secret SOE mission behind enemy
lines and then held hostage for the
safety of Nazi leaders.

Pen &
Sword

AVIATION

First published in Great Britain in 2018 by
Pen & Sword Aviation
an imprint of
Pen & Sword Books Ltd
47 Church Street
Barnsley
South Yorkshire
S70 2AS

Copyright © The estate of Hugh Mallory Falconer, 2018

ISBN 978 1 52672 183 9

The right of Hugh Mallory Falconer to be identified as Author of this
work has been asserted by him in accordance with the Copyright,
Designs and Patents Act 1988.

A CIP catalogue record for this book is available from the British
Library.

All rights reserved. No part of this book may be reproduced or
transmitted in any form or by any means, electronic or mechanical
including photocopying, recording or by any information storage
and retrieval system, without permission from the Publisher in
writing.

Printed and bound in England
By TJ International Ltd, Padstow, Cornwall

Pen & Sword Books Ltd incorporates the Imprints of Pen & Sword
Archaeology, Atlas, Aviation, Battleground, Discovery, Family
History, History, Maritime, Military, Naval, Politics, Railways,
Select, Transport, True Crime, Fiction, Frontline Books,
Leo Cooper, Praetorian Press, Seaforth Publishing,
Wharncliffe and White Owl.

For a complete list of Pen & Sword titles please contact
PEN & SWORD BOOKS LIMITED
47 Church Street, Barnsley, South Yorkshire, S70 2AS, England
E-mail: enquiries@pen-and-sword.co.uk
Website: www.pen-and-sword.co.uk

Contents

Foreword		vi
Introduction		vii
Chapter 1	The Turning Point	1
Chapter 2	SOE	5
Chapter 3	In Tunis Gaol	10
Chapter 4	Tunis to Berlin	26
Chapter 5	The Prinz-Albrechtstrasse	32
Chapter 6	Solitary Confinement	42
Chapter 7	The Hostages	58
Chapter 8	Counter Offensive	63
Chapter 9	The Nazi Way	80
Chapter 10	Sachsenhausen to Buchenwald	94
Chapter 11	Buchenwald	101
Chapter 12	The Road to Dachau	113
Chapter 13	Dachau	129
Chapter 14	Innsbruck to the Southern Redoubt	142
Chapter 15	The Southern Redoubt	155
Chapter 16	The Road to Freedom	169
	Epilogue	180
	Glossary of Comparable Military Ranks	189
Appendix 1	Bibliography	190
Appendix 2	Note by Evelyn Campbell Smith (née Falconer)	191
End Notes		201
Map showing moves from Berlin to concentration camps to the Southern Redoubt and Lago di Braies		202
Index		203

Foreword

Evelyn Campbell Smith, née Falconer

It has taken a very long time to produce this unusual book. My father wrote it from memory thirty years after the end of the Second World War whilst he and my mother were living in Rhodesia. Tragically he then contracted inoperable lung cancer and died early in January 1980.

My sister and I flew out to Rhodesia on the very first direct flight from London to Salisbury since UDI to attend the funeral and help our mother prepare for a return to Britain. We met the publisher who explained that the book would have been printed in South Africa but times had become too uncertain for him to promise anything.

My mother was given back the one (!) copy of the manuscript and later that year returned to England bringing it with her. For some reason she refused to let anyone see the manuscript for the remaining twenty years of her life so it was not retrieved until we were preparing to sell her house.

My sister and I began to put the book on to computer as the original was on the thinnest airmail paper, typed on an ancient typewriter and needed some revision. It took time, we were busy women and the years drifted on. Sadly my sister died very suddenly in 2007 with the book still nowhere near ready for publication.

It was my cousin and 'family historian', Elizabeth Summers, who pointed out to me that I was now my father's last hope of being published. She deserves our gratitude, as do all those mentioned in the book, because the events my father talked about should not be forgotten and are part of the archives of a very vicious war.

Introduction

In spring 1943 the Germans began their retreat from Stalingrad. By then it was also clear that the campaign in North Africa was lost. Some of their leaders began to consider the possibility of final defeat and how to survive as individuals in unmolested comfort. Hoarding cash reserves in Swiss and South American banks presented no problem and was done. Several weeks after the end of the War in Europe two German submarines turned up in Buenos Aires with cash, gold ingots and jewels. In exchange for these the Nazis were to be given hundreds of Argentine passports and identity cards. But ... how to get out of Europe?

The Allies, particularly Lord Vansittart, had made it plain that once Germany was defeated her leaders would be called to account for their acts, not as soldiers or politicians, but as criminals. The Nazis' dilemma, therefore, was not so much acquiring the wealth but rather how to be free to enjoy it.

The method chosen (one with which we are today only too familiar) was the holding of hostages. Some suitable retreat would be prepared, impregnable against any attack except from the air. In the last days the German leaders would take refuge in this stronghold, into which the chosen hostages would have been previously transported. It would be garrisoned by the Waffen-SS divisions which, under the direct order of Reichsführer Heinrich Himmler, would withdraw there in good time, leaving their colleagues in the regular army to carry the can. The presence of the hostages would be a guarantee against air attack and those same hostages would be the currency with which the Nazi chiefs would bargain for life and liberty.

The Nazis seemed to have a rather odd conception of who could be valuable as a hostage. Furthermore, the disruption of communications in Germany during the last weeks of the War made it impossible for junior

Gestapo officers to seek guidance from above. How were they to sort the sheep from the goats in the various concentration camps throughout the country? So they played safe and took the lot – and a very peculiar assortment we were.

Chapter 1

The Turning Point

I remember very clearly the day on which I was supposed to die.

I was tired and half starved, numb with cold, and it was raining – a dreary drizzle. When the truck drew up at a small quarry and I was told that I was going to be shot, the small flicker of hope which I had nurtured since I was captured was brutally extinguished.

Oddly enough I have practically no recollection of my thoughts at that moment. I believe I was past caring and my mind must have been more or less a torpid blank.

I do recall the Gestapo interrogator asking me, for the final time it seemed, if I would give him the wireless code – and my telling him in effect to get stuffed. I do not flatter myself that this was high courage. I was just so miserable, physically and mentally, that I wanted to get it over and be done with everything.

Then, after minutes of standing in the chill rain, I was ordered back into the truck. The pseudo firing squad climbed in behind me.

My only feeling was one of despair that this bleak, squalid life was going to drag on after all.

It was quite some time after I was shoved back into my cell that I suddenly realised that hope, however miniscule, was back again. Was it man's involuntary striving for survival, whatever the circumstances? I can only say that I was aware, once more, of the urge to prevail and not to give in.

During the night I awoke and lay thinking for some hours. It seemed that I had been given back what I had fully believed was to be violently taken from me. My bunk was uncomfortable, true enough, but I might in fact this night have been instead a corpse in a sodden makeshift grave at the bottom of a nameless Tunisian quarry.

This, I suppose, proved to be a lesson of sorts for the future. Never again was I to reach that depth of submission to despair which I had plumbed the previous morning.

I was not, of course, to know this on the night of my reprieve. At that particular stage I did not dare to contemplate the future so I thought of the past – how and why I had landed up in this situation.

In April 1940 I joined the Royal Air Force as a Pilot Officer Rear Gunner. Why I did this I cannot tell. It may have been the genes of my military ancestors; it could have been patriotism; perhaps it was just anticipation of the question 'What did you do in the war, Daddy?' Maybe it was something of each for (at that time) I had nothing particular against Germany even if Hitler did seem a bit of a bounder.

At this point I should explain a little of my past life to make it easier to understand what followed and why I became an "improbable hostage".

At the age of eleven I was taken to France by my mother and went to a French *lycée* for a year. Later, after a more orthodox English education, I went to the Royal Military Academy at Woolwich and from there was duly commissioned into the Royal Signals. A year or two later, becoming bored with Army life in England, I handed in my papers, went to France and joined the French Foreign Legion as a Private (Second Class) for a five year term.

I spent the next few years as a Legionnaire and wireless operator in North Africa using the skills I had learned as a schoolboy in France and in the Royal Signals. This was one of my happiest periods as I enjoyed the life, played plenty of rugby football and came to know well parts of North Africa, particularly Algeria.

Invalided out halfway through my term with knee problems, I married a Frenchwoman. We lived in England where I worked as a professional engineer in the cement industry. When war broke out in 1939 I found that the cement industry was regarded as a reserved occupation so it took me till the beginning of April 1940 to wriggle out of it and join the RAF.

At the same time my wife, whose knowledge of English was still minimal, returned to her parents in northern France with our baby daughter.

Who could have foreseen the bypassing of the Maginot Line and the occupation of France?

I set out for the Bombing and Gunnery School at West Freugh in Wigtownshire. My only memory of that journey is that I was instructed to travel in civilian clothes, thus saving the RAF the cost of a first class ticket.

Probably because of my fluency in French I was then posted to 50 Wing in France just as the German Blitzkrieg began, only to find them installed in a little village five kilometres from Péronne where my wife was. But this bit of luck was not to last for two days later the whole family – together with thousands of others – joined the streams of Belgian refugees jamming every road to the south. Having just set fire to the Péronne airfield petrol dump after filling a three-ton lorry with all the cans it could carry, I happened to be passing the house as they were loading up. I was therefore able to fill my father in law's tank and give him as many cans as he could accommodate. We then crammed the remaining space available in his car with all the wine from his cellar, for it seemed a pity to leave it for the Germans.

As for me, having been sent to 4 Squadron in Lille to give them their evacuation orders, I decided to stay with them for I found the atmosphere more congenial than the pomposity of 50 Wing.

4 Squadron, which was Army Co-operation and fully mobile, was ordered to retire to any suitable field (and almost any field was suitable for Lysanders) in the vicinity of Saint Omer and I was put in charge of the road transport.

It took us nearly ten hours to cover the eighty-odd kilometres from Lille to Saint Omer for every road leading to the south was packed solid with refugees in cars and lorries, on bicycles, in horse drawn traps and farm wagons and on foot pushing handcarts. To get our forty vehicles across was, every time, a nightmare operation and, to make things worse, the Luftwaffe was consistently machine gunning the refugees to keep the roads jammed and so hinder the Allied retreat. It was then that I began to hate Nazi Germany.

We arrived in Saint Omer just in time to refuel and, after seeing off our remaining Lysanders, pushed off again towards Dunkirk. Indeed, the Squadron Commander and I, who had stayed behind to set fire to the petrol dump, left the field to the north as two German motor cyclists emerged from the woods to the south.

Despite its horrors, for us Dunkirk had two redeeming features: the beautiful weather and my father in law's wine. We passed the time enjoying the former and drinking the latter until we were taken off the beaches in a destroyer.

Once the Battle of Britain was over life became very dull. There was nothing for an Army Co-operation Squadron to do but patrol our section of the east coast from Flamborough Head to Berwick upon Tweed and carry out exercises with the Army. I stayed with 4 Squadron until November 1940 and was then, again because of my French, posted to 309 (Polish) Squadron as Bombing and Gunnery Instructor – once more Army Co-operation and Lysanders. While this was not dull, for the Poles were delightful people and adventurous pilots, it was not war and in 1941 I joined the Special Operations Executive (SOE).

Chapter 2

SOE

They stood as signals to the land
Each one a lovely sight.
Samuel Taylor Coleridge

My first days in Special Operations Executive (SOE) were spent at Grendon Underwood in Buckinghamshire, ostensibly to be trained as a wireless operator before being dropped in France as a saboteur. However, when I revealed my considerable experience in the French Foreign Legion both as an operator and as organiser of wireless networks, my rôle was altered.

I was transferred to the Signals Section and at once found myself deeply involved in working out codes of practice for wireless operators behind the enemy lines. We concentrated on developing unsuspicious procedures, the foxing of enemy direction-finding equipment and the selection of cyphers. It was then that I devised the 'deliberate mistake' idea which was later to save my own life.

There was at that time still a lively possibility that Hitler might do a deal with General Franco and march down through the Iberian peninsula to invest Gibraltar. Had he done so it was by no means certain that the Germans could have captured the Rock. There would in fact have been no need for them to try for the fortress could be neutralised and its harbour made useless from the Spanish hills to the west and north. Even more important, with heavy artillery at Tarifa at the southern tip of Spain the Royal Navy could be denied access to the Mediterranean so that no convoys would get through and Malta would fall.

SOE's plan was that our men in Lisbon and Madrid would organise cells of saboteurs to harass the German lines of communication, should they move into the peninsula. My job was to train their wireless operators and lay on their contacts with Gibraltar where we already had an embryo Signals Section.

I flew out of England in civilian clothes – first stop Lisbon – where I organised the Portuguese cells of saboteurs. At the beginning of January 1942 I reached Gibraltar and established my Signals Section on an operational basis then set off for Madrid to repeat in Spain what I had already done in Portugal.

This Signals Section was a peculiar one. My command as Squadron Leader consisted of:

- One lieutenant and six staff sergeants (Royal Signals) as operators
- One corporal (Royal Engineers) to look after the diesels supplying our emergency power
- One Spanish Communist masquerading as a Free French sergeant (in civilian clothes for some reason which now escapes me) who was a highly skilled radio engineer and maintained and serviced our receivers and transmitters.[1]

By the summer of 1942 there appeared to be no further threat to Gibraltar by land but preparations had begun for Operation TORCH, the Allied invasion of French North-west Africa. We therefore turned our backs on Europe and concentrated our attention in the opposite direction.

The American equivalent of SOE was the Office of Strategic Services (OSS). At their request we had already established agents in Casablanca and Algiers, as well as one in Oran. All of these were in direct contact with Gibraltar.[2]

In August 1942 I was summoned back to London to co-ordinate my signal plans with the American Army signals. My job was to ensure that when TORCH was launched the right lights would be flashed from the shore at the right places and at the right time to guide the invading troops to their landing places. We were already more or less geared up for this, the only additional requirement being the establishment of agents in Bône and Tunis which we achieved without trouble.

It is satisfactory to be able to record that all these guide lights shone out on time and in the right place. The one exception was Tunis where, fortunately, it was decided at the last minute not to make a landing after all. It was my intention after the end of hostilities in North Africa to find out what had gone wrong but, when I arrived in Tunis, I was in no position to do so.

However, before the landings took place I had a serious problem. The secrecy surrounding the plans for TORCH was such that no inkling could be given to my agents of their true function. As a result it was difficult to keep up the enthusiasm of operators who took a chance every time they used their transmitters and therefore exposed themselves to discovery by enemy direction-finding equipment. Why, they began asking themselves, were they sticking their necks out?

My agents could not be used as sources of information for, although our enemies knew that an invasion force was preparing, they did not know where it was to strike. If they learned that intelligence was being gathered through clandestine agents in French North-west Africa unfortunate conclusions could have been drawn!

Taking into account that my agents were in no danger of discovery while receiving, but only when transmitting, I gave them regular war bulletins compiled from the BBC. In this way the agent was only at risk during the few seconds of establishing contact and acknowledging receipt, and the viability of the links was confirmed at each contact. Although sent in code these bulletins would reveal nothing to the enemy, even if the code were broken, other than that the British or somebody were putting out propaganda in secret to somewhere. They could not even deduce for which countries these transmissions were intended for we were careful not to use directional aerials.

The Vichy newspapers in French North-west Africa were singularly reticent about Allied successes, which were now beginning to mount up against U-boats at sea, on land in North Africa and in the air over Germany. My bulletins kept up my agents' interest, enabled them to acquire merit by passing on the news to their friends and kept them in practice using the code, while limiting their transmissions to contact and acknowledgement.

One day before TORCH zero hour my agents were told of their real raison d'être and how they were to help. By that time the battleships *Renown, Rodney* and *Duke of York* and the aircraft carriers *Furious, Formidable* and *Victorious* were already manoeuvring in the approaches to Corsica, Sicily and Sardinia in order to convince the Germans that the target of the invasion fleet was one of those three. It is interesting to note that Mussolini and Ciano were convinced that the invasion was headed for French North-west Africa, but they were overruled by the Germans.

The operation was a complete success. Ninety thousand men with their arms, equipment and vehicles were brought thousands of miles by sea, landed dead on target and ... I was out of a job.[3]

With nothing now to keep me in Gibraltar I thumbed a ride with the Navy to Algiers and looked around for something to do.

For a time I helped to recruit and train young Frenchmen who were to be infiltrated behind the enemy lines as saboteurs to help the war effort. While Montgomery and his Eighth Army were sweeping relentlessly westwards across North Africa, the Americans with Anderson's First Army, who were supposed to be moving eastwards, were well and truly bogged down in every sense of the word. From the time of the TORCH landings the rain had seldom stopped and the ground they were on was a morass.

Eventually it was decided that I should land behind the German lines in Tunis with two of my lads (Corsicans who knew Tunis well) and a radio transmitter/receiver in a suitcase. We would see what we could do to harass the enemy.

From *The Secret History of SOE: The Special Operations Executive 1940–1945*, William J.M. Mackenzie, St Ermin's Press, 2000

1 pp.323-4, '... in July 1941 a remarkable figure, Squadron Leader 'Mallory', arrived to give training in W/T. 'Mallory' was an Englishman who had served in the Foreign Legion, a wireless technician and a hustler, known in the service as the 'human bomb-shell'; incidentally a diarist of merit, who has left a very lively account of

his Mission. In about six weeks (while ostensibly 'waiting for an air passage') he managed to establish a wireless set in the Embassy at Lisbon and to train operators for the two SOE 'Circuits' as well as for the Legião.'

2   p.324 'From Lisbon Squadron Leader 'Mallory' went on to Tangier, taking with him an operator to be established there. Even after the Spanish seizure of the International Zone in November 1940, Tangier continued to be something of a diplomatic no-man's land, and SOE was able to indulge in more exciting activity there than in Spain and Portugal. Originally the Mission was in part aimed at French North Africa, and it established various lines of contact across the frontier: but here the Americans were far better placed than we, as they possessed a network of consuls with full bag facilities, and the hand was left to them to play once OSS began to operate at the end of 1941.'

3   p.325 'From Tangier Squadron Leader 'Mallory' passsed to Gibraltar; and the wireless station which he established there in the Rock was probably SOE's most important contribution to history in North Africa: it carried all the clandestine signals traffic which preceded 'Torch', as well as all operational messages during the first days of the operation in Algeria – all other communication broke down. His narrative of its construction is a minor classic in the working of 'Système D', in his case a nice blend of French and British techniques of military 'wangling'.'

p.533 SOE's Part in TORCH 'The success of 'Torch' was conclusive proof (if proof is needed) of the military value of good 'underground' preparation. ... SOE's part was purely ancillary, but in one respect vital .... the entire burden of secret communications with North Africa was borne by Squadron Leader 'Mallory's' station at Gibraltar from General Eisenhower's arrival on 5th November until two or three weeks after D-Day. The American signallers failed at first to solve the technical problem of establishing wireless communications from the Rock to North Africa, and important messages were still carried by the SOE station long after the Allies were established in Algiers.'

Chapter 3

In Tunis Gaol

All that we know who lie in Gaol
Is that the wall is strong
And that each day is like a year,
A year whose days are long.
Oscar Wilde

Towards the end of January 1943 I landed at night with my two companions on the coast of Tunisia behind enemy lines, wearing civilian clothes and carrying my wireless transmitter in its suitcase.

The landing was a terrifying business made, after a fast trip from Malta, from a motor torpedo boat. This vessel was propelled at enormous speed by three Packard aircraft engines which made one hell of a row. The lieutenant, whose pride and joy this vessel was, assured me that the secrecy of our landing would not be compromised by the noise because the boat could run at reduced speed on one engine only which could be silenced.

Sure enough, we crept into land with no more than a murmur from the machinery and we paddled our canvas dinghy ashore to a completely deserted landscape. However, as soon as we were safely disembarked and had sent the agreed torch signal back to the MTB, it turned and headed out to sea with a shattering roar, all engines flat out with a phosphorescent wake which could be seen for miles. Fortunately this performance appeared to arouse no curiosity on the part of the local inhabitants. I think there must already have been so many inshore reconnaissances carried out by naval patrols that this one elicited no special interest.

Having with some difficulty evaded various sentries and patrols, we entered Tunis on foot and were promptly caught in the curfew, thanks to the positive but quite erroneous information I had been given in Malta that there was no curfew! At least we were without the suitcase which we had prudently hidden before entering the town. The military patrol, as was their custom with civilian prisoners, handed us over to the Gestapo.

To be taken prisoner of war, in *uniform*, must be to experience frustration, disappointment and probably resentment at the forced inactivity to come. For an agent in civilian clothes caught behind the enemy lines and in the hands of the Gestapo, there must be an additional and predominant sensation – fear.

Even today, long after it has ceased to exist, the evil reputation of the Gestapo, its pitiless methods and its ruthless cruelty are remembered with horror. Later generations who know little of those times nevertheless associate the word 'Gestapo' with oppression and terror. No Jewish child is left ignorant of an organisation which relentlessly and systematically murdered not thousands but millions of men, women and children whose only offence had been to be born Jews.

For three days I was left in a cell with nothing to do but ponder on my predicament.

The cell, which was about five paces long and two wide, was all in concrete except the door which was steel. Half the floor space was taken up by a concrete bench intended to serve as a bed and in one corner there was a bucket accessible to the tenant and removable from outside through a hatch. The window, about two feet square, was high up in the wall opposite the door, heavily barred, without glass and quite out of reach. It was dark and gloomy, the walls ran with damp and there was a constant draught between the door and the window. There were two threadbare blankets and that was all.

It would be foolish to pretend that my reflections could be anything but terrifying. The Hague Convention offered no protection to people like me who were caught behind the enemy lines in civilian clothes and obviously up to no good.

There had been previous occasions in my life which had been fraught with considerable danger but there had always been something, however feeble, I could do about it. When under enemy fire I could shoot back and hope to hit the other chap before he hit me. On the beaches at Dunkirk or in an enemy air raid I could take shelter and hope that it would be effective. In any case I had known that I was not personally the enemy's target. Usually such periods of risk never lasted very long and there was always a reasonable hope of survival. In my dark, damp cell I was left to acknowledge that I was, personally and individually, in the enemy's sights and that there was nothing that I could do about it. There seemed to be no hope at all.

The first twenty-four hours seemed like an eternity – an eternity of black despair. Then all of a sudden I realised that there was, after all, one tiny spark of hope in the darkness because there was really no reason to suppose that the Gestapo thought me to be other than the Frenchman I had declared myself to be.

So I concentrated on how to persuade the Gestapo that I was not only harmless to their cause but indeed friendly. I must try to give the impression that I myself was so sure of my innocence that my immediate release could only be a matter of course; that any impending interrogation would be merely a friendly chat; that with a merry quip and perhaps even a shake of the hand I would be led to the gate and speeded on my way. How successful I would be I could not of course predict, nor was I at all certain that I had either the ability or the nerve to perform the rôle I had chosen but, in the absence of any other plan, it seemed the only thing to do. At least it could not make matters worse.

How to do this, the line to take and the attitude to adopt had the priceless virtue of giving me something to think about other than my desperate situation. To some extent it even helped me now and again to forget the dank and gloomy discomfort of my cell. It kept my mind busy and fear more or less in the background.

On the fourth day I was taken to the prison office where an officer of the Gestapo (whom I never heard addressed by his colleagues other than as 'Max') was sitting behind the desk.

I think I had never before been so keyed up as I was at that moment for I believed that my life depended on the outcome of this interview. He made no move when I came in which I saw as a good thing, having no wish to be thought important. I did, however, sit down uninvited in the chair opposite the desk as I wanted to seem at ease and with nothing on my conscience. I gave him what I hoped was a happy smile and wished him good morning.

I was much relieved by his opening gambit for it showed that he thought I was a Frenchman and my whole strategy was based on this. He also spoke French extremely well so we were not going to have a language problem. He led off with the questions I had hoped for: what was my name, where had I come from, why was I out during the curfew, what did I do for a living and so on. Above all, where was my identity card?

I maintain that the Gestapo made a mistake in making me a present of three days in which to think things out and lay plans, but it is quite possible that Max had other victims to cope with before getting round to me. Whatever the reason, I was thankful for that invaluable interval.

So – I came from Algiers. I had no identity card because the American Military Police had raided the café where I was playing cards with my friends, taken my card and told me to collect it from their headquarters next day. I had been afraid to go for it because I had heard that the Americans were conscripting civilians for labour gangs and making them work very hard for inadequate reward and I had no desire to toil for people to whom I had taken a great dislike and for very little return .

I said that, finding the Americans unpleasant, domineering people who as soldiers would surely be no match for the Germans, I had crossed the lines by night to be on the winning side. I could hardly be expected to know about their curfew regulations, and I thought it a bit hard to be locked up in a damp and depressing cell before I had even had a chance to account for myself. I added that, now that everything was satisfactorily explained, we could let bygones be bygones and please could I go?

But it was not to be as easy as that.

Max wanted to know all about me: where I was born, where I went to school, where I had been in North Africa and a lot more ... but I had my story ready. When I was at school in Poitiers, at the age of eleven, my mother had had to go back to England for a couple of weeks during which I stayed with the Protestant pastor. He had a son, Pierre, of almost exactly my own age whose identity I now borrowed. Fortunately, whilst in the Foreign Legion I had travelled fairly widely in French North Africa before the war so I was able to talk about Casablanca, Rabat, Marrakesh, Oran and so on without any risk of being tripped up.

I was called back to Max's office several times during the next week and we went through all the same questions again and again, no doubt to see if I would contradict myself. This was when – for the first time but certainly not the last time – I found that solitary confinement had after all certain advantages. I could concentrate without interruption on what I had said, down to the most trivial statements, and make quite sure that I had everything off pat for next time.

All was to no avail and my more optimistic hopes were dashed for I was just left in my cell. But my spark had become a tiny little flame.

There was little doubt that either the First or the Eighth Army would overrun Tunis in the near future and I would be released. Therefore my policy was to lie low, avoid drawing myself to the attention of the Gestapo and hope that they would think of me (if they thought of me at all) as just one of their sixty-odd French prisoners. Most of them were quite harmless to the Reich and were only kept locked up because it was not the custom of the Gestapo tacitly to admit to a mistaken arrest by letting the victim go.

My problem now was boredom and I set about dealing with it. I needed something to occupy my time and the answer was irritatingly to hand: lice.

The popular belief that it is impossible to get rid of lice without benefit of insecticides is wrong. All you need is plenty of time and that was what I had. I had been given two threadbare blankets seething with insect life. These had obviously been used by previous guests of doubtful social status, so I was lousy. Lice can be killed by squashing between the thumbnails. If there are several, you do it several times; if there are thousands, you do it thousands of times. Then, for a brief interval, there are none. After that the next generation hatches out and the thing to do is to kill them before they reach the age of puberty. Then there really are none.

The two tiers of cells, in one of which I was the sole tenant, faced a blank wall of considerable height with a door in one corner leading into the prison yard. For most of the day this door was shut and we were on our own. Communication between prisoners (which was not officially encouraged) was by shouting. When a French warder came in and protested, he was curtly invited to mind his own business and stop interrupting his betters, which he did. But he was not so invited by me; I was drawing no attention to myself at all. The warder could of course have complained to the Germans and retribution would have been swift. However, I suspected that he was not so dim as to fail to realise that the Allies were now drawing closer every day. Consequently, when the Germans were gone and the prisoners released an informer could find himself in a very unpleasant spot.

Our meals, which came twice a day, consisted almost invariably of a small piece of stale bread and some hot water containing sliced carrots. By counting pieces of carrot and comparing the scores it was established that the distribution was fair but niggardly, averaging twenty pieces per citizen per meal. It also appeared that the equality of the sexes was recognised and the women had as much (or as little) as the men. I can confirm that, contrary to the theory plugged by the RAF, carrots do not improve night vision. They are also a vegetable of which one tires quickly.

Counting carrots, killing lice as long as they lasted and listening to other people's conversations were the only diversions in a humdrum existence – until the Gestapo found my suitcase. As it contained passport photographs for the identity card I had not had time to obtain, there was little point in denying it was mine. I declared my British name, rank and number and noted that from then on the Gestapo treated me with a good deal more respect .... but ... seeing that the suitcase also contained the wireless transmitter/receiver ... there was no comfort to be found in this. My poor little spark of hope was utterly quenched.

Inevitably the misery of fear without hope took charge. I was now known to the Gestapo as a British officer caught behind the enemy lines in civilian clothes and with the most compromising equipment possible.

The receiver on its own would not have been so bad, but the transmitter was fatal. My fate seemed certain.

When I undertook the mission which was to lead to my capture I was fully aware that I would be going outside the law as represented by the Hague Convention. If caught I could only expect to be shot. I suppose that a pessimist would simply refuse to embark on an enterprise of this nature unless he were a very brave man. On the other hand, the great majority of those who accepted such a risk were (like me) optimists. They expected to be successful and any thought of the consequences of capture were, if they ever arose, thrust firmly aside. The discovery of my true identity by the enemy was therefore the most crushing possible blow.

On previous occasions when my life had been at risk I had never really appreciated the fact until the episode was over. I do not think that this was due to lack of imagination. It was far more that my mind was so occupied with planning, preparation and subsequent action that there was little time for such thoughts. I realised it afterwards, of course, and probably called myself all sorts of fool and swore never to do such a stupid thing again. Still the episode was over, the worst had not happened and my faith in my luck had received another boost.

Now the case was different. There was no planning to be done, no preparation, no action – especially no action. There was nothing to occupy the mind. All that was left was the sickening realisation that the risk had become fact and that death was relentlessly at hand.

The days that followed represent that period of my life which I would most like to forget. I would like to say that I buoyed myself up with thoughts of dying for my country (*dulce et decorum est*) but I am afraid this was not the case. I was just plain miserable and this was the only time in my captivity which later led to nightmares.

The only possible respite from despair was sleep but sleep is not easily achieved when one's only bed is a threadbare blanket on damp concrete. The cold would seep into my aching bones with no relief even when I changed position. My stomach was gnawed by hunger.

For me there was no release in sleep and the days and nights dragged by in an interminable purgatory of discomfort and hopelessness. I tried to persuade myself that after death there would be no more hunger, no more pain, no more cold or damp and no more fear. But I found no consolation in this at all. I wanted to live. I wanted to see my wife and daughter again and the Cotswolds in Spring and the lights of London and Paris. There were so many things I wanted to do and see.

I was thirty-two years old and I wanted the rest of my life. I did not want to die.

At last the interrogations were resumed and this, unlikely as it may seem, brought a measure of mental relief. Now at least I had something to think about, trying to analyse the trend of the last session and to forecast the course that the next could follow.

The interrogations now took place at all times, morning, afternoon, evening and sometimes in the middle of the night for now the Gestapo were getting their teeth into something very different from some anonymous Frenchman. A British officer, presumably a member of the Secret Service, was a different kettle of fish altogether – particularly with no Hague Convention to limit their efforts.

These interviews were always held in the prison office and I came to hate and dread the place. Whether the irregular times were to suit the convenience of Max or designed to break my nerve, I could not tell. If the latter, they came very close to succeeding. Indeed, I think the saving factor was vanity. The fear of torture (constantly threatened) was always there although in fact it was never used. Nor, to my knowledge, was it ever resorted to in that prison because I believe Max was convinced that he could, by mental cruelty, more elegantly achieve his purpose.

The Gestapo naturally tried to squeeze out of me information concerning the organisation, personnel and so on of the 'British Secret Service' but, to my surprise, they did not seem particularly upset by my refusal to talk. It was when I forced open a cupboard in the Gestapo Headquarters in Berlin after the end of the War that I discovered their reason: they knew it all already!

In fact the information they had got from two captured agents in 1939 was about Military Intelligence (MI) from which SOE was quite separate but, no doubt because the nefarious equipment with which I was caught consisted only of a radio transmitter/receiver they thought I was a member of MI and not a saboteur. But they were doggedly insistent that I should reveal the code to be used with the transmitter.

From my point of view this was no problem for (as mentioned before) I had an arrangement with my base that should this very contingency arise the code could be blown. All genuine messages contained a deliberate coding error and if this should be omitted my friends would at once know that I was acting under duress. Should they wish they could then use the channel to supply the Germans with misleading information for as long as the latter were prepared to buy it.

After the first dozen or so sessions with the Gestapo in my true status, I realised that if I looked hard enough there was once more a tiny little flicker of hope. For one thing, I was still alive. For another, Max kept assuring me that if I would only give him the code I would not be shot. On the other hand, having got the information they wanted, why should the Gestapo bother to keep me alive? I would be much less trouble to them underground. It was indeed a tiny flicker, but I clung to it desperately. If they got something out of me that they thought was of real value, they just might keep me around as something to boast about – which they could hardly do if they killed me in spite of their promise.

It seemed, therefore, vital to convince them that they had got hold of something really hot; too facile a capitulation on my part could easily lead them to suppose that there was a catch in it as, indeed, there was. I decided that it was simply a question of digging my toes in for long enough, but not too long.

In the event, I overdid it.

It happens to everyone from time to time that one thinks 'I'll put it off for one more day' or else 'It'll stand just one more'. And this is what I did, just once too often – or so it seemed. For on the following morning I found myself in front of a firing squad.

I was not particularly dismayed when I was loaded into a lorry with a posse of armed SS men for I had no idea where we were going or for what purpose. There had, for example, been none of the standard formalities which books lead us to believe to be the inseparable preliminaries to execution. I had had no breakfast before we set out, nor had I been offered a cigarette or a glass of rum.

The destination was the quarry which I have described at the beginning of this book, my companions the ostensible firing squad and Max, the Gestapo interrogator.

I thought that the end for me had come; and by that stage, I was past caring.

But the fine art of torture, as practised by the Gestapo, had a long way to go yet.

The routine was repeated the next day with a distinct lack of enthusiasm on the part of all concerned (it was raining again). I clung grimly to the thought that it did not happen last time and it might not happen this. Whether it was something in the attitude of the SS men who shared the back of the truck with me I cannot tell, but I do remember that I just did not believe that my end had come. I also remember wondering if my clothes would ever be dry again and thinking that, after not being shot, it would be a bit of an anti-climax to die of pneumonia. I remember thinking that the firing squad looked as miserable as I felt, even if better dressed and better fed.

It seems odd that the Germans should have tried this intimidation – twice on successive days – with no interrogation in between. The second time could not possibly have the shock effect of the first, particularly unreinforced by further threats. I think Max, who was nobody's fool, must have been acting under the orders of someone of higher rank but inferior intellect. In any case, whoever decided on the repeat performance was no psychologist.

However, this seemed the right moment to give in about the code. If the Gestapo thought they had now broken my nerve, they would presumably be satisfied that they had indeed extracted something of importance. So, trying as hard as possible to look both ashamed and reluctant, I let them have it.

At this point the Germans showed that they knew their stuff, at least as far as wireless operators were concerned. The set was installed, the aerial was put up and then I was given a coded message to transmit. What was in it I had no idea. The whole object of the exercise was for a German operator to listen to my Morse sending so that on future occasions he could copy my style. (Manual Morse transmission is almost as individual as handwriting.) As soon as I had finished sending I was bustled back to my cell and no doubt the German took over. Whether they ever made contact I do not know. In any case it can have been of very little benefit if they did, for the days of the Heeresgruppe Afrika in North Africa were already numbered.

There followed a period of waiting. Living conditions were slightly improved in that it rained less and it was not so cold. There were even days when the sun shone, but not into my cell as the window was too small and the walls too thick. Occasional distant gunfire suggested that the Allies were closing in on Tunis and, had the Gestapo still thought me a harmless French civilian, I would have reckoned my chances of survival as good. As it turned out, even then I would have been wrong.

As it was, the prospect was pretty grim. It was to be supposed that when the Germans capitulated all available space in aircraft would be required for senior officers, for they had no other escape route, and the Gestapo would certainly not be left out. There would equally certainly be no room for me. The civilians, I supposed, would just be left in the prison and would be quickly released but it seemed most unlikely that I, an acknowledged British spy, would be left to start again somewhere else. The only thing to keep my little flame alive was the hope that in the final confusion (for I assumed that flight from the enemy must be accompanied by confusion) there might be either the possibility of escape or of mixing with the civilian prisoners who would be left behind. Yet this hope was indeed forlorn and frustrated misery was once more my portion.

It was during this unhappy time that I developed the philosophy which was to keep me sane for the next two years and it may be well to explain it at this point. It dictated the approach to life and to my captors which I was to adopt throughout the remainder of my captivity, which might otherwise be interpreted as that of an unimaginative buffoon, with the mentality of a not very bright schoolboy, too stupid to appreciate my peril and too insensitive to be cast down. As things turned out, it saved my life.

This philosophy was based on four precepts:

The first of these was that until I was actually dead there was still hope. After that it would not matter any more.

The second was that fear, being a thought process, could at least theoretically be kept at bay by thinking about something else.

The third was that, now that my true identity was known to the Gestapo, my chances of survival were very slight therefore whatever I said or did could not make matters worse and might even, however remote the possibility, make them better. Even if being obstreperous contributed nothing to my safety at all, as it very likely would not, the planning of it would occupy my mind for at least part of the time and that would be pure gain.

Finally, the fourth precept was that, however unlikely the opportunity or insignificant the result, it was still my duty to harass the enemy whenever occasion should arise.

I was dealing with people and until the end it was with people that I would have to cope and against whom, if my philosophy could indeed ever be exercised, my wits would be pitted – more specifically, Germans. So, what did I know of Germans and the German character?

I had only met one German before the war, a fitter sent over to deal with a recalcitrant machine his firm had supplied. He was an admitted Nazi and inclined to be arrogant in his cups – but that is not peculiar to the Germans. He was at first critical of the British in general and engineers in particular, but completely changed his tune after a few acid remarks from our Works Engineer.

Then I remembered *Elizabeth and her German Garden* and a novel by the same author called *The Caravaners*. She was an English lady who had married a Baron von Arnim and in her books described the petite noblesse of Prussia and Pomerania as she had known them. It seemed that Germans had a very great respect for rank and the nobility, to the extent of subservience on the part of the lower orders and arrogance on the part of those more fortunately placed. This seemed to be borne out by the (to my mind) exaggerated deference which Max displayed when in the presence of one of his superiors who visited us during an interrogation, and even by his change in attitude when he discovered that I too was an officer and of higher rank than he.

I was not to know until much later, and at the time it was probably just as well, that I was unpardonably arguing from the particular to the general. I was subsequently to meet and get to know many Germans of great dignity, integrity and courage, whose conduct and general behaviour were beyond praise.

Were all Germans fanatical Nazis? I was sure they were not. Information had reached us from occupied countries that the Gestapo and their colleagues the SS under the command of Reichsführer Heinrich Himmler were responsible for arrests, persecutions and atrocities of which the Wehrmacht (the armed forces) by no means approved. In short, there was no love lost between the Wehrmacht on one hand and the Gestapo and the SS on the other. A situation could arise where this fact could be useful.[1]

These were things I knew, or thought I knew, about the Germans. It remained to formulate some plan of action – perhaps only a plan of attitude – for whatever future remained to me.

I began by deciding that (not least to keep up my own morale) I must try never to be the underdog – at least psychologically; a prisoner no doubt but never under the spiritual dominion of my captors. That sounded very grand and theoretical so what did it really mean? It simply meant that I would have a line of thought to pursue, I could plot and scheme however futile the end result and so thrust fear into the background or so I hoped.

In Germany it seemed the underdogs were those without rank or position. Squadron Leaders are more or less two a penny in almost any air force, so the alternative seemed to be blue blood, of which I had not very much. At least this would be a bluff the opposition would have some difficulty in calling. It would have to be blue blood in what I thought was the German style: arrogance, underlined by rudeness and emphasised by obvious contempt for the party of the second part. I was not then to know that this was a most slanderous conception as far as a great many Germans were concerned.

An opportunity arose not long after I had formulated this policy to put it to trial. Shortly after the code episode I was called quite unexpectedly for another interview – so unexpectedly that I had no time to transfer my watch to its usual hiding place in the top of my sock. After tidying up a few points Max asked to see it and I had no option but to hand it over. It was a rather nice one I had bought in London in 1940 from which the name of the makers (Hughes of Fenchurch Street) had been skilfully erased, leaving only the legend 'Swiss movement'. After looking at it and listening to it tick Max dropped it into his pocket. This annoyed me so much that it was not difficult to be truculent in spite of my unhappy plight and it took very little effort to embark on the new policy. I made a very caustic remark on the subject of the Gestapo's reputation for pillaging, obviously well founded. It was a great relief to see that Max looked more embarrassed than angry and, my daring greatly enhanced by this fact, the conversation went something like this:

Max   'It is my duty to make sure it does not contain a compass.'
Me   'Put it on the table to see if it points North.'
Max   (After trying this futile experiment) 'I also have to see that it does not contain a map.'
Me   'It goes, doesn't it? It's full of machinery, not an atlas.'
Max   'I shall look just the same.'

With that he got a pair of pliers out of the drawer and screwed off the back of the watch. He then stirred up the machinery with the tip of the pliers and handed it back with the remark that I could see that the Gestapo were honest people in spite of what I had been told.

Max certainly came out top in that particular argument but his action had one significant effect; how significant I did not at first realise. My fear of the Gestapo was now overlaid with hate, a much more positive sentiment, and a measure of contempt for a man in his position who could be so childish. I am convinced that this trivial incident went far towards giving me confidence in the policy I hoped to pursue. Also, as I thought back over our dialogue when I was back in my cell I was sure that, if he had thought I was an insignificant French civilian, he would have flown into a rage, real or assumed, at my first remark. It is true that he had his revenge but it did seem as if arrogance was not entirely without effect.

I supposed this episode and the firing squad sequence came under the heading of mental cruelty and I added a fifth precept to my philosophy: mental cruelty does not work if the victim is aware of what is intended. I was later to find that it could be effectively applied in reverse – by the prisoner on his keepers.

My basic hope now was that the Gestapo would keep their promise and hand me over to the regular forces as a PoW. In this I was disappointed and it was fortunate for my relative peace of mind that I did not know at that time that such a move would have been quite unprecedented. I was later to discover that particularly persistent escapers from PoW camps were occasionally passed over to the Gestapo for safer keeping, but I never heard of a transfer in the other direction.

Life now returned to its tedious normality; even the lice had been liquidated and no longer provided a diversion.

Then one day something happened which was entirely without precedent. A barber set up shop in our alley and cut all the men's hair. At the same time there was a strong rumour, originating from one of the French warders, that we were all to be taken to Germany. It seemed that the Gestapo were fussy about the appearance of the merchandise they handed over to their colleagues in Europe. This all seemed to me very unlikely for, if the Germans were really with their backs to the wall, it was difficult to believe that a nondescript collection of French civilians and a British spy would be given priority in aircraft over German personnel who must be very badly needed in Russia.

But it was no false rumour.

Next morning we were all lined up in the prison yard under the eye of Max himself who, it appeared, was in charge of the convoy. There was no weeding out of prisoners to be taken and ones to be left. They just took the lot. I now believe that this was due to plain inefficiency and a failure to plan ahead for, as I shall relate, exactly the same thing happened in Germany in April 1945.

By now the Allies were very close, the sound of gunfire was clear to the south and to the west and it was bitter indeed to be removed from the scene when rescue could only have been a matter of a very few days. It must have been more bitter still to all the French men and women in our party who had never done anything to warrant arrest and who, as it turned out, would never know freedom again.

We were counted, signed for, loaded into open lorries and driven to the airport where a fleet of Ju52 transport aircraft (three engines and the fuselage apparently made out of corrugated iron) was standing ready for take-off. For the journey to the airport I had been chained by the leg to the oldest prisoner in the party, a bald-headed old man who could hardly walk. This is a great deal more effective than a ball and chain for one does not worry about hurting a ball and chain.

After a period of argument, shouting and confusion in this case caused by the protests of numerous German officers who felt that they had a better claim to the transport than a lot of scruffy civilians, such was the might of the Gestapo that we were taken and they were left.

Chapter 4

Tunis to Berlin

Some vessel of a more ungainly make.
Omar Khayyam

We eventually took off and headed north to the sea at about five hundred feet.

The aircraft itself was just an empty shell inside, the crew consisted of pilot and navigator and there was no visible armament at all. There were also no seats and the dozen or so prisoners sat on the floor. An ordinary kitchen chair had been provided for the solitary SS guard who, armed only with a rifle (not a very suitable weapon for use in a confined space), would have been easy to overpower, particularly as he was a martyr to airsickness.

I was chained to the airframe and it was disturbing to note that no other prisoner was so chained. I tried to console myself with the thought that this was not because I was someone special but merely that, being in the RAF, I might be expected to try and hijack the aircraft. The fact is that it would otherwise have been relatively simple for us to seize control and fly it either to Malta or to First Army territory in North Africa, but the Gestapo had presumably foreseen this possibility and taken suitable precautions.

As far as air attack was concerned the machine was a sitting duck. There must have been considerable blind spots below and astern and, at five hundred feet, there was very little scope for evasive action. In addition the Ju52 was hardly designed for aerobatics. There was no fighter escort and it seemed that the aircrews were either singularly devoted to duty or, like the Gestapo, very eager to leave Africa.

The flight as far as we were concerned was uneventful but miserable for the airsick SS man who spent the whole trip clasping a bucket with his rifle abandoned beside him. It was thoroughly frustrating for, even if my French companions had overpowered him which they could easily have done, it was impossible to undo my handcuffs and nobody else could fly the plane. The key to the cuffs was with Max and he was not with us.

My two Corsican companions were not in the party either and I was afraid that they had been liquidated by the Gestapo as not worth keeping. It was inevitable that I should wonder whether at some later stage an official more senior than Max would reach the same conclusion about me.

We flew north-west over the coast, turned nearly north over Palermo and four machines landed at Naples airport after an uneventful flight. Here everybody disembarked except me. There followed a long wait while our four guards and the reception committee searched the sky, with increasing anxiety, for the missing aircraft. They waited in vain for, as I later discovered, out of the considerable number of planes which took off from Tunis these were the only four to survive the trip. I never saw Max again.

The immediate problem was how to get me off with no key. Eventually a Feldgendarme turned up with a bunch of keys, one of which fitted, and I was at last able to join my companions.

There was a further wait for the others but in vain for they, with all their prisoners, were at the bottom of the Mediterranean. Knowing how many millions died miserably in concentration camps between then and the end of the war, who shall say that they were not the more fortunate?

From the airport we were eventually moved in lorries to an hotel in the town where we were parked in the basement. We were also fed and, while the peacetime clients of the hotel would no doubt have complained bitterly about the cuisine, for us after weeks of Tunisian carrots it was in the five-star class. For the first time I realised that a party of hungry prisoners is made up of two sorts of people: those who share with others they believe to be in greater need than themselves, and those who furtively seek to get more than their due. In the last days of the war (my next experience of communal living under difficulties) I saw this again to the discredit of people whose need was not pressing and who considered themselves to be of a social status superior to those whose food they sought to appropriate.

Apart from eating we sat around on boxes, waiting and speculating, and trying to keep up our spirits by mutual encouragement. This was not entirely successful.

We knew the Germans were collecting forced labour from occupied countries. Enough letters had filtered through from France to Tunis for us all to be aware that, were this to be our fate, our lives would be intolerable and our survival unlikely. For the first time for weeks we were not in solitary confinement and, with few exceptions, we were determined to subdue our apprehensions by assuming a cheerfulness it would have been difficult to justify. We soon had an opportunity to forget, at least for a little while, our more gloomy thoughts by acting in concert to discomfort the enemy. With nothing to lose, we let ourselves go.

Our arrival in Naples had obviously been expected but it seemed that we can only have been announced as a 'party of prisoners including one British officer'. Had all the aircraft arrived, including the one with Max on board, this would of course have been all that was necessary but there was still no sign either of him or of our companions. Eventually the Gestapo officer who had met us at the airport turned up and started drawing up a nominal roll of his own. This was our chance.

Accurately to register by name some fifty people in a confined space who will not keep still is, at the best of times, difficult. When the majority of these people are French, with whom it is instinctive to hamper rather than assist any official in the execution of his duties, it is very difficult indeed.

For example, he had a man wearing an overcoat and a beret down as 'Marcel Duval' and a bit further down another chap in shirt sleeves called 'Duval, Marcel' and he had not even been told a lie.

A delightful old lady became two delightful old ladies by turning her black coat inside out, for it had a red lining. The changes in appearance which one French girl could achieve by manipulation of her headscarf were remarkable.

At the end of the first attempt the officer had at least six more people on his list than there were in the room, and this seemed to give him the impression that he was losing prisoners all the time, possibly through a hole in the floor. He was offered a flood of advice in torrential French, all of it unhelpful and some of it anatomically impossible which, since he did not speak French, added to the confusion. It eventually took him the best part of an hour, and half a dozen SS men as marshals, to balance his accounts. This first insight into Gestapo lack of imagination, at least in the lower echelons, was to be of great help in my subsequent forward planning.

At about six o'clock in the evening, when it was still broad daylight, we were taken to the railway station. This time we had to walk going two by two like a girls' school crocodile but with considerably more guardians than even the strictest ladies' seminary would have thought necessary. The civilian population seemed a great deal more sympathetic than could have been expected from Germany's principal ally. It also seems that I was seen in this procession by an Italian working for the British who reported my presence to his contacts, and this was the last news of me that SOE had until I turned up in London in May 1945. I was chained to the same poor old man as before, whose decrepitude obviously singled him out for the ball-and-chain act. I never saw him again after we reached Berlin and I cannot believe that he could have survived whatever rigours were in store for him.

At the station the Naples–Berlin train was waiting, and the Gestapo took over a coach by the simple expedient of throwing its occupants out on to the platform. Wherever they went they certainly influenced people but I doubt if they made many friends. Pursuing my policy of arrogance I complained that, as an officer, I had the right to travel first-class but this got me nowhere except into a third-class carriage the same as everybody else. In the compartments we sat four a side – three prisoners and an SS man in the window seat – and three more SS men patrolled up and down the corridor.

We were also issued with bread and sausage for the journey, which the improvident had eaten before the train pulled out. As soon as darkness fell I was again handcuffed to my old man, which was not conducive to a restful night for either of us. Our desires to change position never seemed to coincide and handcuffs, particularly when used to join two people together, restrict movement more than the uninitiated would believe possible.

The night was long and I could not sleep. My philosophy of making plans for the future to keep my mind off more immediate and more distressing subjects just would not work for I had no idea at all what lay ahead. It was obvious that our departure from Tunis had been notified to the Gestapo in Naples, otherwise there would have been no reception committee. It was equally obvious that I had been specially mentioned, for a British officer was expected, but how much other information about me had been passed on I had no way of knowing.

Did the non-arrival of Max mean that he had been shot down between Tunis and Naples and my dossier with him? He had certainly had a bulky briefcase with him at the airport, but had copies been sent by another hand?

I was still chained but did this mean that I was particularly wanted by Gestapo Headquarters, or just potentially dangerous because of my military status?

Even if my dossier was lost with Max, surely he would at least have sent a signal to the Prinz Albrechtstrasse to the effect that he had caught a British officer in the Secret Service. Or would he?

So many questions to which I did not know the answer.

Since I had not been liquidated in Tunis I tried very hard to believe that, as promised by Max, I was on my way to a PoW camp. I sought to persuade myself that the Gestapo had notified the Wehrmacht that I was on the way and that they kept me fettered simply because they did not want to take the risk of me escaping and making them lose face. But there were PoW camps in Italy and the destination boards on the train ominously declared that it was heading for Berlin.

It must have been a very slow train for it was morning before we stopped in Florence. This was the highlight of the trip. Some ladies, no doubt the equivalent of the Women's Voluntary Service in England, came along the carriages with ham rolls and coffee in paper cups and, surprisingly, we were allowed to accept their offerings. I can only suppose that the Gestapo thought that the ladies would assume that we were voluntary workers going north but, to judge by their generosity and murmured sympathy, they were not deceived. One lady gave me two little cards, like cigarette cards, one with a picture of a Florence bridge and one of the Lungarno which I kept throughout my captivity.

Night fell as we climbed the Brenner Pass and just before dawn we were in Munich. Here again ladies came along the train with coffee, but it was a brew very inferior to what we had been given in Florence, and there were no ham rolls and no sympathy.

Late in the afternoon we reached Berlin. My fellow prisoners were loaded into lorries and driven away while I, with two guards, was kept waiting at the station entrance. With a flicker of hope I began to think that perhaps, since I was not intended for the same destination as the others, we were just waiting for the army to come and take me over but this was soon dashed for the car which eventually turned up was manned by three members of the Gestapo.

It was still light enough as we drove through the town to read street names and, as we turned into the Prinz-Albrechtstrasse and started slowing down my heart sank, for this I knew to be the address of the Gestapo Headquarters. I went into that sinister building in utter despair.

It was at least a relief when we got inside to be taken up to the first floor rather than down to the notorious cellars. (In fact I never did go down there either during or after the war for, when I revisited the place in July 1945, the building was in ruins and the cellars blocked with rubble.) We went along a wide corridor, through a door which had to be unlocked from the inside when my escort rang a bell, and I was thrust into a cell with a big, heavily-barred window, a bed, a cupboard, a table and a chair. Free at last from the handcuffs and exhausted by emotion and a sleepless night, I mercifully slept until morning.

Chapter 5

The Prinz-Albrechtstrasse

*Questioning is not the mode of conversation
between gentlemen.*
Samuel Johnson

The next day started with a mug of the liquid which, in wartime Germany, was amusingly called 'coffee'. I believe it was made from roasted barley and its only virtue was that it was hot. But water was brought in a bowl and I was able to raise my wilting morale by shaving for, when we left Tunis, the Gestapo had returned to me my wireless suitcase – without of course the wireless – but with the personal possessions it had contained.

I was then left alone.

Since leaving North Africa this was the first time I had been on my own with an opportunity to try and appreciate the situation, and I lay down on the bed to think. My position seemed pretty hopeless for, even if the Gestapo Headquarters respected the Hague Convention for the treatment of prisoners of war (and I had no reason to suppose that this was the case), as far as I was concerned it did not apply. I had not been taken prisoner in uniform and on the field of battle.

I had been caught behind the enemy lines, in civilian clothes, with a highly compromising suitcase, falsely declaring myself to be a Frenchman in sympathy with the German cause and patently prepared to do it as much harm as I could.

On the other side of the ledger was the fact that I had already been twice in front of a firing squad in Tunis, which had turned out in each case to be a bluff in very poor taste in my view. But that had been to frighten me into revealing the code, which I had done, and having achieved their purpose the Gestapo had doubtless kept me alive while making certain that the code worked. I could only hope that resistance in North Africa had collapsed before they had time to find out that they had been sold a pup. This did indeed seem likely for otherwise they would presumably have been after my blood, instead of which they had just left me alone.

I began to wonder whether in the last days of German resistance in Tunis they had just shipped off the entire contents of Tunis gaol because they were in too much of a flap, or too much of a hurry, to sort out the sheep from the goats. So the sorting out was to be done in Berlin – but I had been sorted out for I was already separated from my erstwhile companions and therefore some sort of information about me must have reached Berlin. But how much? The Gestapo in Naples had obviously not known a great deal about me other than that I was some sort of British officer. Did Headquarters in Berlin know more? I could not possibly tell, and my only hope was that Max had not shown up in Naples. It was just possible that if he had been shot down so had my dossier.

Yet I was back to square one all the same for if my dossier was in fact in Berlin or enough of a report had been sent by signal there was no valid reason, legal or otherwise, why the Germans should go to the trouble and expense of keeping me alive.

My philosophy for the preservation of sanity had never before been put to a more severe test than it was now. Indeed, its only tenet which seemed to be in any way still valid was that while there was life there was hope – and I was still alive. It was more than ever essential that if I were not to go mad I must have something to think about other than my presumably impending fate. If I could concentrate on making plans to meet whatever alternatives the future might conceivably have in store for me fear could, at least to some extent, be driven into the background.

What alternatives could there be?

The first was that the Berlin Gestapo knew all about me and would want to see if there was anything else to be squeezed out of the orange before it was thrown away. Yet though Max had certainly boarded one of the aircraft clutching a fat briefcase he had never appeared since, so there was a very fair chance that he and my dossier were at the bottom of the sea.

The second alternative was that the Gestapo did not know all about me and would want to find out more.

The third possibility was that I was simply at a staging post on the way to a PoW camp.

The first alternative did not bear thinking about. The third called for no particular planning on my part, so the one to concentrate on was obviously the second: that the Gestapo did not know why I was there.

I had to convince the Gestapo that I was a British officer and nothing else which would at the very start call for an explanation as to why I was in civilian clothes and not in uniform, and also why I ever came into the hands of the Gestapo to start with.

I settled down to some intensive thought.

My first interrogation was brief. A tough looking Gestapo officer and a rather seedy looking civilian sat together behind a table and I was invited to sit down facing them. The first thing I noticed was that there was no dossier on the table and my hopes rose. I was asked a few general questions about name, rank and number, refused to give the details of my squadron or of the aircraft I was allegedly flying, and the interview was over.

It really did look as if my dossier was at the bottom of the Mediterranean and that the Gestapo in Berlin had no idea why I was in their hands. This meant that I must make an all-out effort to convince them that I was just an aviator who had been shot down and all they had to do was to pass me on to a PoW camp. The trouble was that I was in civilian clothes.

In most squadrons in North Africa, at least in the RAF, anybody could have gone flying in almost anything they chose, but what about the Luftwaffe? From the little I knew of Germans I imagined that, if anyone could permit himself such laxity, it would be a member of the upper crust ('If I do it, it must be all right.'). So I had to be the upper crust and I was back with the idea of pulling rank and pretending to blue blood. The rank, such as it was, was no problem for presumably the Germans had copies of the RAF List and could check my name, rank and number, but the blue blood called for very careful planning. The Gestapo certainly had their copies of *Burke's Peerage* and *Debrett*, which not only list the nobility and gentry but also give considerable detail about the ramifications of each family.

If, therefore, I gave a name, I would surely be caught on the first couple of questions. I must, therefore, refuse to reveal my alleged pedigree and a good pretext seemed to be that my presence in enemy hands could embarrass some relative in a high place; and I must try to underline my pretensions by arrogance in the Prussian style, or what I thought to be the Prussian style.

I reckoned it would be wise to try out my histrionic powers, or lack of them, on the warder and the opportunity came next morning.

As I lay on the bed pondering these things and realising that my almost complete ignorance of the German language was not going to help, the door opened to the usual clashing of bolts and an SS man came in with some printed form which his duties apparently required that he should complete.

He was very upset to see me lying on the bed.

'Aufstehen,' he yelled, 'das Liegen ist verboten.'

'Verboten' I could understand; the rest I could guess.

'Speak English,' I said, without moving.

To my surprise he backed out and shut the door, to come back a few minutes later with one of his mates.

'Sleep is forbidden,' said the newcomer.

This was it – I could try the arrogance now or for ever hold my peace. I thought of a couple of adjutants I had known, and of a certain Regimental Sergeant Major.

'I'm not asleep. What is your rank?'

'Unterscharführer.'

'What's that in a civilised army?'

'Sergeant.'

This was the moment or never and I thought of the RSM. I sat up and tried to look disgusted, and took a deep breath.

'And I am a major. STAND TO ATTENTION, YOU HORRIBLE MAN!'

To my astonishment – and considerable relief – he drew himself up and clicked his heels.

'And you,' I snapped, pointing at the warder, and he too stiffened to attention.

They both looked shaken but, had they only known, not half as shaken as I was as I struggled to maintain what I hoped was a haughty look. I lay down again on the bed.

'All right,' I said, 'What do you want?'

The warder with the help of his colleague then set about filling up his form, which seemed to be about age, height and things like that. From the way he peered at me I guessed that colour of hair and eyes came into it too. They then withdrew.

So far, so good. But had I made my point at the right level? To have impressed a sergeant and a private was all very well, but it was hardly likely to influence my future. If they reported my behaviour to higher authority they would be bigger fools than I took them for since they had only to keep their mouths shut and their humiliation by a prisoner would never come out. Something more spectacular and more public seemed to be called for, something that was sure to reach the ears of my interrogators. Meantime at least I had the satisfaction of having apparently carried my point at this low level.

A possible opening came with the midday meal.

This revolting repast, consisting of a bowl of thin, sour soup and a piece of dubious bread, arrived at about noon and was dumped on my table. The soup was cold.

Knocking on the door brought no response so I hammered on it with the chair, and this produced the English speaking sergeant.

'The soup is cold,' I said.

'The kitchen is a long way away.'

'I don't care. I want my soup hot.'

'I regret,' he said, 'that is not possible.'

This was what I hoped he would say. The bowl shot past his ear and hit the wall on the other side of the corridor with a satisfying crash, and the soup slid down to form a nauseous puddle on the floor.

'That's all it is fit for. Now, get out!'

By this time there were several spectators in the corridor and I hoped the incident would get reported to higher authority. Whether it did or not I cannot tell for it was never mentioned again, but I like to think that it helped.

The sergeant withdrew meekly and when, about ten minutes later, he turned up again with a bowl of soup which was no better in quality than the first but was properly hot it was difficult to hide my surprise.

The tone of my next interrogation, which took place the following morning, was markedly different and opened with an almost friendly discussion about the course of the war.

From hopefully claiming that the British and Americans in the west would be unable to gain a foothold on the continent of Europe, and that the Russians had already outrun their strength in the east and would shortly be annihilated, the officer remarked that it would still take the Germans a long time to subdue so large an area as the USSR. It would be more sensible, he suggested, if there were peace now between Germany and the Western Allies, since this could at present be arranged without loss of face to either side, and then the Germans, the British and the Americans could all join forces to rid the world of the menace of Communism for ever. What did I think?

This was as good as an admission that at least this ornament of the Gestapo was beginning to have doubts about a successful outcome to the war as far as Germany was concerned, and my spirits rose accordingly.

I remarked that the Gestapo, as a privileged organisation enjoying the confidence of the Führer, was presumably authorised to listen to British broadcasts – a pleasure I understood to be denied to the German public in general – and they must therefore already have grave doubts about Germany's chances in the present conflict. In fact it was more a question of 'when' they would be finally defeated rather than 'if'.

I also produced the old cliché about Britain always losing the first battle in a war but always winning the last one. As far as I was concerned I had no reason to suppose that Mr Churchill, in whom I had complete faith, would deviate from his declared intention of accepting nothing less than unconditional surrender. With this policy I was in full agreement and, with defeat staring them in the face, the Germans would be well advised to capitulate without further ado, thus avoiding the total destruction of their towns and cities by my colleagues in the RAF and the United States Army Air Forces.

This produced no reaction at all, and the officer changed the subject.

Under what circumstances, he asked, had I been taken prisoner?

Now I was quite sure that my dossier had not survived the trip from North Africa and I could go all out trying to put over the indignant officer act and, if necessary, the blue blood bluff.

'My aeroplane was hit by flak.'

'Did you come down by parachute?'

'No, I made a forced landing.'

'Why are you in civilian clothes?' (The sixty-four-thousand dollar question.)

'I was wearing pyjamas at the time.'

'Was that your usual flying uniform?' asked the officer.

'Not as a rule. We'd had a bit of a party the night before and I'd overslept. I only just got down to the flight in time for take-off as it was.'

'Was that sort of thing approved of in your squadron?'

'Well, no – not really. But it depends a good deal who you are – you know what I mean.'

He glanced at his companion with what I tried to believe was a meaning look.

'Where did you get the garments you are now wearing?'

'One of your colleagues produced them.'

The question I was dreading – why had I been handed over to the Gestapo at all – never came.

'What sort of aircraft were you flying?' asked the officer, not as if he wanted to know but rather as if it were the right thing to ask.

'No comment.'

There was a long pause while the two conferred in German and I would have given a good deal to understand what they were saying. In fact I believe it was at that moment that I determined to learn the language however difficult it might be. In the meantime, I thought I had better screw up the courage to do something in the arrogance line, to back up the bit about 'it depends who you are', and decided to feign boredom.

I examined my finger nails and polished them on my sleeve. Then I got up and wandered across the room and looked out of the window. As this faced on to a brick wall I strolled round the room with my hands in my pockets and contemplated a picture of the Führer. Then, finding a magazine on a table in the corner, I took it back to my chair and started looking at the pictures. Finally, I nerved myself to take a cigarette from the packet on the table and light it with the civilian's matches. I was waiting tensely for the explosion but, to my surprise and profound relief, none came. I have no idea what the pictures in the magazine were about and, for all I know, I could have been looking at them upside down. Then:

'Do you refuse to answer questions?' shouted the civilian. I paid no attention.

'Listen when I speak to you,' he said sharply.

'Are you talking to me?' I asked, looking up.

'Yes, of course I am. Do you refuse to answer questions?'

'There's no need to shout. Yes, of course I do. You've had my name, rank and number, and that's all I'm allowed to give.'

'Very well,' he said, 'we accept that. But you will not object to giving us some details about yourself. For example, what is the rank of your father?'

I hardly dared to believe it. Had the soup incident been reported after all? Or had the crack about the pyjamas registered as I hoped it would? I felt jubilant and, if this seems an exaggeration, it must be remembered that in the wretched situation I had been in for weeks on end, any little ray of hope was a great, big, bright light compared with nothing at all.

'My father is too old for military service.'

'I mean, what is your father's title?'

This was the question I had foreseen which could tear everything up for good.

'I am not prepared to give you any more information at all. I suggest you hand me over to the military authorities for transfer to a PoW camp and save me a lot of discomfort and yourselves a lot of wasted effort. Good morning!'

With that I stood up and walked towards the door, waiting for a blast of rage which never came. Instead, the sentry was called and I was taken back to my cell.

When I am doing something I tend to get completely wrapped up in it and this is certainly what happened during this interrogation. On the way back to the cell I felt quite happy, satisfied that I had done what I had set out to do but, when I was again alone and had time to think, I was appalled.

It suddenly came to me that my rank and arrogance theory was based on nothing more than my own deductions from thoroughly inadequate data, spurred on and abetted by wishful thinking. It now seemed to me that what I had said and done could well rebound on me and that any merciful feelings my questioners might have had at the start had probably been effectively quenched. I now believed that, completely indifferent to my remarks and behaviour, they had just sent me away temporarily while they decided whether to have another go using less elegant methods, or to have me liquidated without more ado.

I lay on the bed and passed some very unhappy hours for I could not then know, and did not discover until (as I shall relate) the following Christmas, that the Gestapo were already on the lookout for promising hostages and that with a completely different and not very intelligent object in mind I had unwittingly picked on the surest way of staying alive.

The same afternoon I was taken by car some twenty kilometres north of Berlin on, I noticed, the road to Stettin. For what was to be the last time I had hopes of transfer to a PoW camp but, when we reached a town called Oranienburg, we turned off the main road and drew up outside a gate, set in a high wall topped with three strands of barbed wire which were mounted on insulators. Over the entrance was the name of the establishment: SCHUTZHAFTLAGER SACHSENHAUSEN.

Sachsenhausen, I knew, was one of the more notorious concentration camps. The first word I was only able to translate later: 'Protective custody camp'. When one recalls that the 'protected' prisoners in this camp were killed off by their 'custodians' at the rate of literally thousands a month, the name verges on the ironic.

Was this, then, the place of execution? It seemed extremely likely. I was convinced that this, at last, was the end. So much for all my cleverness with the Gestapo.

We drove through the camp to an inner enclosure, the Zellenbau, or cell block. There we left the car and went through a small door in a wall also crowned by three strands of electrified barbed wire, into a well-kept garden and on into the building.

This, shaped like the letter T, consisted of three corridors with cells on either side – eighty cells in all – two corridors forming the head of the T and one the stem, with the offices and washroom at the intersection. Here, I was handed over to a man in SS uniform who appeared to be in charge. He led me down the left-hand corridor and ushered me into cell No.74 – my home (although I did not then know it) for the next twenty-two months.

Chapter 6

Solitary Confinement

No arts; no letters; no society;
and which is worst of all, continual fear and danger of violent death.
Thomas Hobbes

My feelings were mixed. It could be that I had been temporarily transferred to what was obviously an establishment run either by or for the Gestapo until Higher Authority had time to decide on my fate – either to shove me in the gas chamber (and so make my cell available for some more interesting tenant) or send me to a PoW camp. Or it could be that I had merely been classified as 'not interesting' and would be forgotten until the end of the war.

I abandoned the PoW hope for, if this had been the intention, it hardly seemed likely that the Gestapo would have let me see the inside of an establishment they could scarcely have wished to have described outside its walls. I therefore pinned my hopes on being forgotten. What was in fact the true situation it would have been impossible for me then to deduce.

Clinging to the 'forgotten' hypothesis, it remained to discover the routine to which my daily life would be subordinate, establish ways of defeating boredom and examine the possibilities of escape.

For me the prospect of further and possibly prolonged solitary confinement held no particular horrors. I was thankful, therefore, to be alone. It was to happen in the future, when my relations with the Camp Kommandant had become sufficiently strained, that I would complain of the solitude just to make sure that, even when the cells were overcrowded and more guests kept arriving, he would seek to spite me by refusing my request for a companion.

The cell itself, about fourteen feet long and eight feet wide, was large enough for comfort. It was furnished with a bed with a straw mattress, a wardrobe for which I had no use, a table and chair, and a bucket with a lid. There was a large window facing south – that is towards Berlin – at the end opposite the door, barred and opening outwards at the top. The glass was clouded to prevent the inmate from seeing outside but by standing on the bed and peering round the edge it was possible to see quite a lot of what went on. There was also a black paper blind to pull down for the blackout.

The door had a peephole in it, closed by a shutter on the outside, but the whole thing could be revolved from the inside so that the shutter fell clear and a little of what went on in the corridor could be observed – rather like looking through the wrong end of a telescope. Later I kept this peephole covered with a piece of paper stuck over the inside to discourage snoopers. This the guards would remove whenever they spotted it and I would immediately replace. As the guards had their duties to perform and I enjoyed complete leisure, the paper was more often on than off and, in the end, the guards affected not to see it.

Beside the door, on the inside, there was a little panel with two buttons marked 'Rufen' and 'Abstellen'. Pressing 'Rufen' caused a bell to start ringing outside the guards' office and this could only be stopped by pressing the 'Abstellen' button from inside the cell. While the bell was ringing a light came on over the cell door so that the guard on duty could tell where to enquire. Since the bell could not be stopped from anywhere but inside the cell in question, the guard had no option but to come and see what one wanted.

I presume that when this camp was built well before the war these cells were intended for important political prisoners. By the time I got there the status of the clientele had dropped considerably, so much so that certain cells were even occupied for short periods by SS men, who were no doubt atoning for some disciplinary peccadillo. This bell system was later to play its part in my operations – as an irritant, as a warning and as a source of electricity.

The daily routine was quickly established. At about eight o'clock in the morning I was escorted to the washroom and, on my return, the breakfast mug of 'coffee' would be waiting on the table. Unless one had saved up some bread from the evening before this was all the breakfast there was. A little later I would be taken to the barber to be shaved. Why we enjoyed this luxury I could never find out. It seemed that there had 'always been a barber' and I suppose that this was another relic of the establishment's palmier days. Like the bell it was presumably considered an essential convenience for the class of prisoner for whom the place was originally built and since then, no order having been given for it to be suppressed, it just went on operating.

This morning procedure was quite a lengthy business starting at 6 am. There were eighty cells and no prisoner was supposed to have any knowledge of, or even catch sight of, any of the others. As a result each one had to be either back in his cell or locked up in the washroom or the barber's shop before another could be let out.

The guards started with cell No. 1 and worked their way through the establishment in numerical order which was why I – in No. 74 – was left until relatively late.

The barber was installed in a cell which had been fitted out with a washbasin, mirror and barber's chair. Karl the hairdresser was a prisoner, a member of that persecuted sect the Jehovah's Witnesses. The German members of the Witnesses had to a man refused to obey call-up orders when Hitler introduced conscription and had been given prison sentences. On completion of their terms they were all picked up by the Gestapo at the prison gates and transferred to concentration camps where, as political detainees, they had been ever since and were likely to remain. Karl was a charming little man, an excellent barber, and with the quiet serenity so many members of this faith seem to enjoy.

Possibly because of their placidity, all the labour employed in the Zellenbau were Witnesses: Karl, Franz the gardener and the man who cleaned out the cells.

Karl spoke nothing but German but it was he who helped me to learn the language, although he was officially forbidden to hold any conversation with his clients. He also became involved, although he affected not to know it, in my future lines of communication.

While one was out of one's cell, either in the washroom or with Karl, another Witness swept it out and emptied the slop pail.

Except on Saturdays, when the Camp Kommandant visited each prisoner, the rest of the morning was free. Lunch – a bowl of wishy-washy soup and a piece of bread – turned up at about noon, and there was then more uninterrupted peace until the evening meal at about six o'clock. This too, was soup of the same quality as the lunchtime fare and accompanied by another bit of bread. On Sundays we had a piece of gristle and potatoes for lunch, and jam or cheese for supper. The cheese was a mystery to me for the label called it 'semi-fat cheese: 0 per cent fat'.

The day ended with a radio programme – not through any kindness on the part of the authorities but just by sheer good luck. On the other side of the cell compound wall, exactly opposite my cell window, was an outside loudspeaker on a pole which was switched on every evening (except when there was an air raid) at about seven o'clock. There was music, once a week there was what I later discovered to be a pep talk by Doktor Goebbels and, at eight o'clock, the news and *Wehrmachtbericht* – the official daily war bulletin from Hitler's Headquarters. This was a great incentive to learn German.

Another daily event, at no fixed time, was the issue of three cigarettes. Alcohol I can take or leave and lack of it worries me not at all but it annoys me exceedingly not to be able to smoke.

Three cigarettes a day are not much but in my early days in Sachsenhausen I was able to get cigarette papers. The arithmetic is this. The tobacco from one cigarette can be used to roll six thin ones (very thin) and the six butts make three more. These three make yet another and the total is ten. It is however wise – should any reader wish to economise in this way – not to make a cigarette out of the butts of the butts. This tobacco, as I found out by personal experience, contains a remarkable concentration of nicotine and is practically lethal. It is much better to blend the old with the new. Later on the tobacco question was satisfactorily solved (to my satisfaction anyway) and did not recur.

On Saturday mornings, as already mentioned, the Camp *Kommandant* visited each cell. This was also presumably a relic of the more prosperous days of the Zellenbau for he obviously derived no pleasure from it and neither did we. No doubt Gestapo Training Part I had not been appropriately amended when the category of prisoner changed so, in his methodical German way, he just carried on with the old routine. Since the Kommandant spoke nothing but German his visits, at least as far as I was concerned, were brief and conducted with distant formality.

Solitary confinement provides ample leisure and its real menace is, of course, boredom. Very few people can sleep twenty-four hours a day, and fewer still can make their minds an absolute blank and keep it that way; it is just not possible to stop thinking.

One of the basic tenets of the philosophy I had evolved in Tunis was, it will be recalled, choice of thought: the effort to push fear into the background by thinking about something else. Fear of the future was, of course, still there. No prisoner in a Nazi concentration camp could, unless he was a moron, view the future with complacency. As far as I was concerned I was concentrating on the belief that I was forgotten rather than in the condemned cell and, as time went on and nothing happened, this did seem to be more and more likely. The focus of thought thus shifted from the relegation of fear to the frustration of boredom.

I gradually realised that the fatal thing to do was to mull over the past. The immediate past was when one was caught and, with the unfair advantage of hindsight, one could think of various ways in which capture could have been avoided. The most depressing thoughts one can have are those which begin 'If only ...'. All thought must be fixed on the future, for thinking of the present is no use at all – not at least when it is the sort of present I was then experiencing. One must be entirely forward looking. A certain amount of time must be spent planning for the immediate future, in order to overcome boredom, and the rest of one's thoughts must be for the more remote future, which will begin with the recovery of freedom and go on from there.

Since this cannot be very realistic, for who can tell what form the future will take, there is an almost infinite variety. Lines of thought can be started, set aside, stored up for future use like hats on a rack and, when boredom threatens, it is only necessary to lie on the bed, cast one's mental eye along the rack and choose the line of thought which seems at the time the most attractive. In two years of solitary confinement you either master the art of selective thought or you go mad and kill yourself – as several of my fellow prisoners did.

Inevitably the first thoughts of a prisoner are concentrated on the possibility of escape. It was not very long before I had to face the fact that, from my cell, there was just nothing doing.

The cell door, which opened outwards, was secured with two bolts and a lock, and the inside was smooth and flush fitting. The whole thing was made of steel.

The window was barred and the bars were set in concrete at fourteen different points.

The ceiling was concrete.

The floor, which was planks over concrete, consisted of boards every one of which ran the full length of the cell and disappeared under the concrete skirting.

The guard was locked in with us at night and had no key to the outer door.

Even if it had been possible to get out of the building under cover of darkness by clobbering him, there was the ten-foot wall surrounding it with three electrified barbed-wire strands on top. This was no bluff for, shortly after my arrival, a prisoner who was being taken out to be hanged, committed suicide by jumping up and grabbing the wire. There was a flash and he was killed instantly.

This wall, as well as the similar one round the camp itself, was under constant observation from a number of watch towers and, except during air raids, was floodlit at night.

There was also a low wire six feet inside each wall, and anybody crossing it was instantly and without warning shot down by machine-gun fire, even if he was an SS man.

Escape was just not possible from this inner fastness.

In the first months, however, I had a task before me which took up all my time: learning German. With no dictionary or grammar this was not without its problems. It seemed to me that if I could get hold of some German text on a subject with which I was familiar it should be possible to get a start. After that it should be progressively easier to increase one's vocabulary as the meaning of words could be more readily deduced from the context.

For sanitary purposes our keepers provided newspaper, neatly torn into squares of a suitable size, so I went through my ration each day and carefully sorted out the bits which contained all or part of the *Wehrmachtbericht*. This I felt was the best subject to choose, for at least I knew what it was about. Progress was pretty rapid, not because of any particular Pentecostal gift on my part, but simply because I had unlimited time at my disposal with no interruptions.

I was at first puzzled by the agreement of adjectives and articles and suffered a severe initial setback because I wrongly inferred that this followed the rules of Latin grammar. It was some time before I realised that it was, in fact, dog Latin – perpetrated, as I later found out, by Martin Luther. Luther was a renegade Roman Catholic priest and when he translated the Bible into German, for which at that time there was no standard set of rules, he used the corrupt Latin syntax to which clergy in the lower echelons were accustomed, and his text became the basis for modern high German.

As soon as I was able to concoct simple phrases I tried them out on Karl each morning, for there was nobody else on whom to experiment. I did not want the guards to know prematurely that I was learning to understand what they said to each other, for one never knew what useful piece of information one might be able to pick up. Sometimes he understood nothing of what I said. Sometimes, very rarely, it was correct. Sometimes it was incorrect but he got the meaning and then said slowly what it should have been. After a time I was able to move from the war bulletins to other parts of the toilet paper and widen my vocabulary and by the end of 1943 I could even understand most of the broadcasts. By Easter 1944 I was fluent, if grammatically inaccurate.

There were other time-consuming occupations. On one of my trips to the washroom I found a rubber band which was a valuable discovery since my cell was full of flies. It is a prep school custom (or it was in my young days) to speed the dragging hours by flicking the earlobe of some classmate in the row in front with a bit of elastic. For killing flies the same method may be used. At first it is rather messy and tends to spread the victims out in a gory splodge on the wall, but precision comes with practice and a trained marksman can decapitate a fly as neatly as may be with no mess at all. At the top of my form I could bring down three out of five on the wing.

I also had a pack of cards, acquired from a companion during the journey from Naples to Berlin, and jealously guarded. I only knew two games of Patience and these I played many thousands of times, keeping a careful record of the results.

For those interested in making a book the odds against winning the first game (called I believe Chinese Patience) are exactly three to one. This may have been weighted in the later stages as the cards wore out and their backs became as familiar to me as the faces. With the other game (Idiot) the odds are about seven to one, success depending on a greater degree of luck.

It occurs to me to remark at this point that, while at all times I took great care to conceal those small objects I did not want to lose – such as my fountain pen which lived in my sock – from the time I was first caught I was never searched. I can only suppose that whenever this would have been appropriate everybody thought someone else had done it already. The fact remained that, had I been armed when first caught, I could have had the weapon yet.

At some time each day when the weather was fine I was allowed to exercise for about half an hour in the garden bounded by two wings of the Zellenbau and its surrounding wall. Surprisingly, since the paths ran just under the cell windows, I was left quite unsupervised during this period and there was no point from which I could have been secretly observed. It may be that the guards thought I could only speak English and, as there were no British in any of the cells overlooking the garden, they could more usefully occupy their time than in watching me loitering round the precinct.

I was thus able to carry on interesting if disjointed conversations with those tenants whose windows looked out on my promenade with whom I had a common language and who were bold enough to participate. It is only right to say that the risk they took was greater than mine, for they could be spied on through the peepholes in their cell doors, whereas I could always see in time the arrival of the enemy through the garden door.

One of my first contacts was the French Minister of State Yvon Delbos, with whom a friendship developed which we were able to renew after the war. Fortunately, by the time my exercise periods had been stopped by the Camp Kommandant as a reprisal, other and more efficient lines of communication had been established.

Since communication between prisoners was forbidden, there was an obvious incentive for me to communicate. There must, I thought, be some reason for this strictly imposed ban and I wanted to know what it was.

The principles of communication between human beings are relatively simple: they are visual, audible or tactile and their exercise is either public, private or secret. For my purposes I would clearly be restricted to visual or audible contacts – that is, writing or sound – and they would have to be secret. To be precise, it would be better if the purport of the message was to remain secret from the SS but, essentially if any message was intercepted, it must be impossible for them to detect either the sender or the addressee or the results could be disastrous.

Visual signals can be either by signs understood by both correspondents, such as Semaphore, or they can be in the form of written messages.

Writing can, of course, also be in code and of this I had had considerable experience, but for present purposes this was not to be envisaged. Apart from the difficulty of establishing a cypher understandable to all parties to the correspondence, there was really no point since the greatest danger was going to be the discovery of the fact of communication rather than the content of any message. Essentially, written messages must be undiscovered in transit and destroyed after receipt; or, if intercepted, it must be impossible for anybody to identify either the writer or the intended reader.

Finally, there was the basic problem of how to produce written messages. I still had my fountain pen and there was a bottle of ink in the barber's shop. Karl was always willing to turn a blind eye if so desired; like that if there was a row he could always truthfully say he had never seen me take any ink. Paper was an insurmountable difficulty until I remembered that potato contains starch. By saving a little of my Sunday ration it was quite easy to stick together strips of margin torn from the ubiquitous toilet paper and make up sheets of any format one might desire.

Audible signals range from speech to a series of noises, again in a form understood by both parties, such as the Morse Code. With audible signals secrecy requires that an outsider is either not aware that communication is taking place, or else cannot understand what is heard. Of the two the first is the more desirable but the second is not excluded provided always, in our case, that the enemy can identify neither the sender nor the receiver.

There remained the question of a code for audible communications which would either be person to person through the cell wall or (conceivably) broadcast along the central heating system, for water pipes are excellent transmitters of sound.

The Morse Code has three disadvantages for general use in prisons.

First, it is not easy to teach under such conditions for it is not at first sight logical. One would expect A to be one dot, B two dots and so on but, for excellent technical reasons, this is not the case.

Secondly, it is difficult to tap the Morse Code as the dots and dashes have to be represented as the interval between two sounds rather than, as originally intended, the duration of a sound.

Thirdly, the Morse Code is international and any of the guards might have learnt it in the army or in the Hitler Youth.

The system we used was simple although time consuming – but then we had plenty of time. A was one tap followed by one tap, B was two and one, C was three and one, and so on up to E which was five and one. F was one tap followed by two taps, G was two and two and so on down to

Z – five and five. This gives only twenty-five combinations so there is no Q, which can easily be replaced phonetically by two other letters. For example, in English one would transmit 'Kwaint' for 'quaint'.

My first correspondent was, as I have related, Yvon Delbos. We were already in verbal contact during my exercise periods and it was no problem to throw a note wrapped round a stone through his open window. As he had a pencil the reply came out, written on the back of my message, within a few minutes.

I set about writing out in English and French the instructions for the tapping code which I bestowed in various pockets ready for slipping to suitable people as the occasion arose.

The first subscriber was my neighbour on my left. I had already had some conversation with him round the edges of our open windows, but this was a risky business. He was a Ukrainian. There had been no opportunity of getting the code to him during the exercise periods for both our windows overlooked the entrance path to the Zellenbau, on the opposite side of the wing from the garden. However, one day as I was being brought back from the barber, the guard leading the way (which shows incidentally how inefficient the guards were for a prisoner should always be escorted from behind), his cell door was open and, as his cell number was 75, it seemed a reasonable bet that he was in the washroom, so the piece of paper sailed in through the door.

No sooner was I back in my cell than I realised that the door might just as well have been open because another guard was in with him for some reason, but fortunately this turned out not to be so, otherwise the whole communications system would have been ruined before it got off the ground and I would have been in really big trouble. As I say, this was not the case but it gave me a big fright and I determined to be more careful in future.

The same evening my neighbour called me up on the wall.

This was the start of a correspondence which was to last for at least eighteen months until he was taken away to another place. His name was Yaroslav Stetzko. Between the retreat of the Russians and the establishment of a German military government he had been Prime Minister of

Ukraine for the week that the country had been 'independent'. A militant campaigner for the independence of Ukraine from Russian domination since his student days, Stetzko had to date spent about a third of his life in various political prisons, mostly Russian. He had been tortured and had been condemned to death a couple of times but had always managed to escape before the fatal day.

Stetzko's neighbour on the other side was a young Russian pilot, Vassili Vassiliev Kokorin, who had been shot down behind the German lines on the Leningrad front. Being Molotov's nephew he had been singled out for special treatment, although at that time we did not know why. He too joined the network, with Stetzko as relay station and interpreter, for Kokorin knew no English or French. Fortunately, he knew the Roman alphabet for my code could never have coped with Cyrillic letters.

And so the network spread. Each new subscriber had two neighbours, one on either side, each in turn an incipient recruit. I did, however, insist that no new member should be enrolled without my specific approval and each had to be vouched for by a reliable sponsor. There were many Germans in the Zellenbau and I wanted no risk of the system being blown by someone trying to curry favour with the Gestapo. The danger was, of course, not so much the matter of being caught communicating as the danger of the SS learning the code and listening in – in which case they could have learnt far more than was good for them, or for me, or for my correspondents.

By using this network I was also able to establish direct contact with certain people through writing. For example, there were four basins in the washroom and I corresponded with four different people by arranging for our messages to be left stuck with soap to the underneaths of the basins – a different basin for each. There were other caches as well and altogether I had some half-dozen friends with whom I was in direct contact by letter. This came in very useful later on when I went into the newspaper publishing business.

As Christmas 1943 drew near one of my Roman Catholic friends, Graf von Halem, remarked in a letter that on what would most certainly be his last Christmas on earth the thing he would miss most would be the Midnight

Mass. Although myself brought up as a Presbyterian, I had always accompanied my wife to Midnight Mass and felt that any religious comfort which was possible in that dismal prison should be arranged. Catholics know their liturgy by heart, there was a bishop to hand, so I determined to do something about it. At my request the Bishop of Lublin drew up a code of knocks, to be broadcast by him over the central heating system to mark the various stages of the Mass, and this I circulated to all my correspondents, asking them at the same time to pass it on to as many other people as possible but without revealing the source. Once again it was taking a risk, but I could not believe that we could suffer disaster in so good a cause.

At about twenty minutes to midnight on Christmas Eve three majestic knocks echoed along the pipes to announce the Introit. The bishop was a frail old man but he had a good wristy action for pipe bashing. The stipulated knocks followed at intervals and, at about 12.15 am a carillon of clangs announced 'Ite, missa est'. I had asked everybody taking part to knock twice on the pipes when the Mass was over and I counted at least twenty-two acknowledgements from various distances and of various strengths. The bishop had a pretty good congregation for what was to be his last Christmas Mass.

There were three *Unterscharführer* (sergeant) guards in the Zellenbau in addition to the man in charge, *Sturmscharführer* (RSM) Ikarius. Two were on duty together each day and the other, in turn, was alone on duty in the building at night. The three guards were Lux, Meyer and Schmidt.

Lux had a lean and hungry look and was above average intelligence for an SS man.

Meyer was a pleasant looking baby-faced blond. Of the three Lux appeared the most dangerous but it was Meyer who was the killer. I think the reason was this. Lux was a little too old to have been through the full gamut of Hitler Youth training but Meyer had certainly had the complete treatment, which included a curriculum it is difficult to credit in a civilised country.

Children were taught that their duty was to the Führer alone and they were required to report to the authorities any shortcomings in others, even their own parents. If this resulted in the arrest and the execution of the child's own father or mother, the acquired merit was the greater. They were encouraged to have dogs as pets and, when a real affection had developed, the child was ordered to shoot the dog he loved. This was called 'training in emotional discipline'. So Meyer was a killer.

Schmidt was much older, one of the lot who had joined in 1933 to get off the breadline, and he was just plain stupid. He was so dim that in an emergency it would certainly take him some time to remember that he carried a gun, longer still to lug it round from the back of his belt where he was in the habit of carrying it and disentangle it from its holster. He could then be relied upon to get in a muddle with the safety catch and would probably have forgotten to load it anyway.

After the considerable noise made by the Midnight Mass celebration I waited with some trepidation to see what the reaction would be of the guard on duty. The puzzling thing was that there was just none at all. After some time I thought it would be interesting to see who was on duty anyway so I pressed the 'Rufen' button, prepared to say that I had leant against it by accident. There was a very long pause while the bell tolled monotonously up the passage, and then Schmidt appeared. He had some difficulty getting the key into the lock but he eventually got the door open and peered in. The reason for his dilatoriness was at once apparent – he was as tight as a tick. I wished him a happy Christmas and added that he had better make the best of it for, according to the war news, his next Christmas was going to be a stinker.

With a noisy hiccup Schmidt admitted that he had never had such a miserable Christmas in his life.

'It's all right for you,' he muttered, 'when Germany has lost the war you'll be back home and happy. But what will there be for me? Just hunger and misery like in 1933.'

'Yes,' I said, 'I'll be all right – just so long as Meyer doesn't pop in here one Sunday afternoon and shoot me in the back of the neck.'

Schmidt hiccuped again.

'You've got nothing to worry about; Meyer won't shoot *you*.'

'Why not?'

'He just won't.'

'Why not?'

'He'll shoot plenty more, but not you.'

'Why me, specially?'

'You and some others.'

This was increasingly intriguing for I had never counted Meyer among my admirers. In fact, he made it perfectly obvious that he hated my guts.

By this time Schmidt had gone a horrible colour and looked as if he wished he were dead. I was terrified he was going to pass out on me before I could get the story out of him so I pulled him into the cell and pushed the door to. It did seem as if his state was due more to terror than alcohol.

'Which others?'

'I daren't tell you.'

'Tell me.'

'I can't. It's a Gestapo secret.'

There was nothing for it but blackmail.

'Do you know that the man in cell number 76 is called Kokorin? And that he is Molotov's nephew? Isn't that a Gestapo secret? Shall I tell the Kommandant about Kokorin and say that you told me? It must be very cold now on the Russian Front.'

'If they find out I've told you I won't go to the Russian Front. They'll hang me.'

'That would probably be better than freezing to death in the Pripet Marshes. Still, there's no need for either. Why don't you just tell me what you know? I won't give you away if you tell me the truth.'

'You are hostages,' Schmidt whispered.

At first I thought I must have misunderstood, but I was pretty sure that 'Geisel' meant 'hostage'.

Eventually it all came out.

Schmidt was not, of course, in the confidence of the Gestapo upper crust, and in any case he was only an SS man, but certain orders had been passed down even to his insignificant level. It appeared that there was a list in the *Sturmscharführer's* office headed 'Sonderhäftlinge' (special prisoners) and Schmidt had heard the Kommandant tell Ikarius, both being of the Gestapo, that these people were hostages. The guards had been warned that under no circumstances were the prisoners on that list to be harmed and that any orders given concerning them were to be carried out, however odd they might appear.

There were four names, one of which was mine, and it took an awful lot of persuading to get the other three. They were Yvon Delbos, Kokorin and Payne Best – the British Intelligence officer who fell into the trap the Germans laid for him at Venlo in 1939.

Having sent Schmidt to try and sleep off his blind before his colleagues came in the morning, I settled down to some very hard thinking. Certain pointers seemed to be significant.

- There was the curious attitude of the Gestapo Headquarters interrogators.
- There was the fact that, when one came to think about it, my hammerings on the wall and the Christmas carillon on the water pipes could not really have been as private as I tried to believe, and yet nobody had done anything about it.
- There was the fact that I was still alive.
- Finally, of the four of us not one was a German.

It all added up: I was a hostage. Why, for what purpose, I could not imagine. The main thing was that, for the first time since I was captured, I knew that my life was not in danger.

Chapter 7

The Hostages

Necessity never made a good bargain
Benjamin Franklin

Αt this time I had no knowledge, of course, of the German Hostage Scheme which I subsequently acquired, some of it after the war was over. It will be appropriate, however, to outline the whole project at this point, not only to make it easier to follow the thought behind events as they occurred, but also to explain the occasionally unusual and sometimes quite extraordinary action of Gestapo officers of junior rank in the closing weeks of the war.

In the Spring of 1943 German successes on all their fronts not only came to a halt but started to crumble. Lines of communication, already stretched to the limit, were severely harassed by enemy action and in at least one case irreparably cut. The supply of equipment and stores and the movement of reinforcements either fell far below the essential minimum or ceased altogether.

In North Africa Montgomery's initial successes were founded on a superiority of armour opposed to Rommel's Panzerarmee Afrika depleted in strength and, through the diligence of the Royal Navy and the RAF, seriously short of fuel and ammunition. The death knell was rung by the Anglo-American landings in Morocco, Algeria and more directly Tunisia in the TORCH operation of November 1942. The Heeresgruppe Afrika capitulated at Tunis in May 1943.

On the Russian front disaster crowned the German penetration of the USSR with the capitulation of Field Marshal Paulus and his Sixth Army at Stalingrad at the beginning of February 1943 – a capitulation which was only delayed until then by Goering's unfulfilled promise to supply the beleaguered German troops by air.

From then on, the German forces embarked on retreat from the east, the south and in 1944 from the west – a process which, with the exception of one abortive spasm in the Ardennes, was to continue without interruption to culminate in their utter destruction in May 1945.

Two German fanatics, Hitler and Goebbels, were still furiously insisting in January 1945 that Germany would win the war – I heard them myself over the Sachsenhausen loudspeakers. Since the broadcasts from *Deutschlandsender* were heard by the German troops on all fronts (they were issued with receivers tuned to that wavelength but which could not receive the BBC), the daily war bulletins inevitably had to be accurate. Even Goebbels, with all his eloquence, could not deny a retreat in which many thousands of his military audience had actually taken part. The most that could be done was to delay the announcement of disasters but even these tactics seldom served any useful purpose.

Yet, in January 1945, with the Russians on the Oder and the Western Allies on the Rhine, Hitler and Goebbels were still steadfastly declaring their faith in a German victory with, as their only talking point, vague references to secret weapons about to be launched against the Allies.

Goebbels underlined his conviction and reinforced his exhortations to the very old and the very young to join the *Volksturm* (Home Guard) by assuring the German public that, were Germany to lose the war, so dreadful would be the future of their country that he personally would ensure that neither he, his wife nor his children would survive. And that is what he ultimately did.

It seems that Goebbels really believed, even in 1945, that Germany could still win in spite of everything – but did Hitler? We will probably never know.

Others, however, as far back as the Spring of 1943 were already far from convinced that a German victory was certain or even probable, and decided to take measures accordingly. The problem was to ensure not only survival in case of defeat, but survival in liberty and comfort.

Money was of course a simple matter to arrange. Very considerable sums had already been moving out of Germany and the occupied countries into bank accounts in Switzerland and South America.[1]

Having arranged for the disposition of the cash, it remained to make sure that its owners would stay at liberty to benefit from it. It was inconceivable that the Allies would take no action against the leaders of a country which had murdered in cold blood, and under atrocious conditions of misery and terror, millions of people whose only crime against the Reich had been to be born Jews instead of Gentiles; which had corrupted its own youth and sought to corrupt the youth of the countries it had occupied; which had ruthlessly attempted by imprisonment and death to suppress every instinct of patriotism in the countries it had conquered; and had pillaged the art treasures of most of Europe.

The solution they chose was to bargain for their freedom with the hostages they would hold. So, to their record of murder, rapine, corruption and pillage they added kidnapping. They had nothing to lose.

The bargaining would have to be done from some place which could not be overrun while negotiating – which called for a fortress and a garrison.

The garrison was ready to hand without any need to call on the army proper, a step which would have been at the least distasteful to the Nazi leaders and, such was the ill feeling between the politicians and the General Staff, probably abortive. They would use the Waffen-SS, the armed divisions of the SS, commanded by Himmler.

For the fortress they chose the Puster Tal, a valley in the Dolomites. Isolated by the precipitous flanks of those remarkable mountains, there are very few passes into the valley from the outside world and those that exist are easy to defend. Trenches, fortifications and tank traps were built across these side valleys and it is to be supposed that ammunition, stores and food were to be concentrated there in good time. Whether this was in fact done I do not know, but we were certainly to see nothing of the food. This was the *Festung Sud*, the Southern Redoubt.

It is a matter for speculation which of the Nazi leaders were involved in this scheme for survival. I doubt if Hitler had knowledge of it and Goebbels surely had none.

Goering was in on it for he was the only one who actually went into the Southern Redoubt, only to leave again when the SS never showed up.

Himmler must have been one of them for only he could have arranged for the Waffen-SS garrison.

Todt may have been brought in to organise the defence works, but he died in 1943.

In any case it was most unlikely that there were more than a dozen founder members of this exclusive escapers' club as there were probably no more than a dozen top-rank Nazis who could trust each other anyway with the tacit admission that they already looked on the war as lost.

As I knew from the unhappy Schmidt, certain hostages had already been selected before Christmas 1943. With the four in Sachsenhausen, others had been marked down in other concentration camps:

Stevens (Payne Best's fellow dupe at Venlo)

Pastor Niemoeller in Dachau

Peter Churchill (because of his name although he was in fact no relation) still in Fresnes prison in France

Léon Blum and his wife in Buchenwald

Chancellor Schuschnigg and his wife in Flossenbürg, I think, at that time

Various others.

It seems certain that trusted Camp Kommandants, such as Kaindl in Sachsenhausen, Kramer in Auschwitz and Koch in Buchenwald, had been briefed to watch out for a certain category of prisoner, though probably not entrusted with the full plot. My own selection was undoubtedly the result of the high-handed line I had taken in the Gestapo Headquarters.

The curious feature was the quaint idea the Nazis appeared to have had of the sort of people the Allies would be interested in.

They held several Russians: Kokorin and Stalin's son in Sachsenhausen (but Stalin's son committed suicide on the electric fence before the war was over) and General Bessonov – though the Russians would never admit that any Russian prisoners of war existed.

Prince Philip of Hesse was included, who was admittedly some sort of cousin of the British Royal House – but still a German who had been a Gauleiter and a party member.

Prince Xavier of Bourbon was there – but the French Royal House is in exile.

They found a Colonel Jack Churchill and optimistically added him to the squad – though he too was no relation of the British Prime Minister.

Then, after the abortive conspiracy and attempt on Hitler's life on the 20th July 1944, they added the families of the conspirators.

Finally, in the confusion of the last days some very odd characters indeed were either accidentally included or climbed on to the wagon of their own volition.

Taken all round, I reckon we were a pretty useless bunch of hostages.

Chapter 8

Counter Offensive

*What the De'il hae we gotten for a king
but a wee wee German lairdie?*
James Hogg

Until 2 am on Christmas morning 1943 my activities had orig-
inated in the combat against boredom and had expanded as a
result of simple curiosity. They were, however, overlaid with an
element of danger.

I was assuming that the Gestapo had lost interest in me and that I
was just forgotten. If this were so I was running the risk, if detected, of
reminding some unfriendly authority of my existence. I was, therefore,
extremely careful. If, on the other hand, I was the mouse in some cat
and mouse act, due for elimination when someone got round to it, I had
nothing to lose – but this angle I tried to forget.

Now the whole situation was changed. I was a hostage, apparently
inviolate, and it seemed that I could stick my neck out with impunity. I
therefore went back to what had, at the time, seemed the most futile of
my Tunis resolutions: to harass the enemy wherever possible.

Obviously I was in no position to start a shooting war and anything
I tried would have to be on a strictly psychological plane, which seemed
to me to be limited to the promotion of pessimism about the outcome of
the war. This appeared from the existence of the hostage scheme to be a
matter of intensification rather than creation – and mental cruelty.

Mental cruelty was a thing which the Gestapo prided themselves on
doing rather well but at which they were, in general, not very good for
they tended to confuse terrorisation by threats with the more insidious
art of innuendo called for by the subtler approach.

As I had already realised in Tunis, if the victim is aware that mental cruelty is intended, it must (by its very nature) be without effect – it may irritate but it cannot dismay. As far as I was concerned there was now an effect which was to incite me to examine the possibility of retaliation in kind. The obvious person to start with was the Camp Kommandant for I thought that by taking it gently and observing his reaction, I could perhaps tell how far it was safe to go.

The Camp Kommandant was a skinny little half portion called Kaindl. I have probably spelled it wrongly for I never saw it written down. When I first arrived in Sachsenhausen he held the rank of *Obersturmbannführer*, which I estimated to be the equivalent of lieutenant colonel, and was subsequently promoted to *Standartenführer* (colonel) for exceeding the quota of deaths he was required to bring about per month. He was a Gestapo man.

As I have already related, he visited the cells every Saturday morning in the course of his regular duties and, as far as I was concerned, these calls had so far been restricted by language difficulties to the briefest of salutes. Now, however, I decided that my German was fluent enough to warrant having a bash.

The next visit started off as usual.

'Guten Morgen,' said the Kommandant.

'Guten Morgen,' I replied.

So far, the old routine. This was the point at which, after a glance round my cell, Kaindl was accustomed to withdraw, accompanied by Ikarius, the RSM. This time I addressed him in German and the conversation went something like this:

'As an officer,' I said, 'I am naturally interested in the progress of the war. How long do you think it will be before Germany is finally defeated?'

He looked at me as if he had had a back answer from a monkey at the zoo.

'I thought you could not speak German.'

'I couldn't.'

"But you've just spoken it."

'I've learned it.'

'Who taught you?'

Ikarius was looking pretty startled too and it was a great temptation to say that he had been my teacher. This, I thought, would be starting too much at one time and I resisted it. I remembered the apparent success I had had with the interrogators at Gestapo Headquarters by taking a snooty line and I was, after all, a hostage.

'It is easy,' I said, 'to learn a primitive language like German.'

Kaindl looked furious and Ikarius horrified and I wondered what I had let myself in for. But, instead of storming out of the cell, the Kommandant took up the cudgels.

'What is primitive about German?' he shouted, up on his toes like a little bantam cock. 'Have you never heard of Goethe or Schiller?'

'Mere amateurs,' I said, 'they copied all their best stuff from Shakespeare.'

This produced no explosion, and I had another thought.

'Schiller was, of course, a Jew.'

This outrageous statement left Kaindl speechless.

'I'm surprised,' I went on, 'that you, presumably a good Nazi, should praise such a man to me.'

Kaindl stormed out of the cell followed by Ikarius and slammed the door in a very uncontrolled way; he never even said goodbye.

To my amazement he was back again on the following Saturday – routine means a lot to the Germans. This caught me off balance with no offensive prepared. It had never occurred to me that he would visit me again, so it passed off with only the usual insincere courtesies on either side.

Since Kaindl was a small conventional man with an equally small conventional mind it was not difficult to plan a conversation from the initial 'Guten Morgen' through to a suitably offensive exit line. All his answers were trite, not to say platitudinous, and there was no problem about steering the dialogue in the right direction so that my final remark was always logical and never a non sequitur. The theme varied but the effect was always the same: that Germany had no hope of winning the war. Kaindl was a glutton for punishment.

The result was inevitable. First my cigarette ration was stopped for three months, no doubt on technical advice, every time I produced my Saturday morning snide remarks and he must have been surprised that this had no restraining effect. When I left Sachsenhausen I had accumulated just on eleven years of 'no smoking'. However, the smoking ban did cause me to go into the blackmail racket.

Then he stopped my daily exercise in the garden but this was also of little importance. For one thing my communications were working so well that I had other means of corresponding with friends whose windows overlooked the garden and I was soon very busy with my newspaper. Also, thanks to the miserable food supplied by the SS, my weight was now down to six and a quarter stone (6.25 stones is equivalent to 87.5lb imperial or 39.69kg, or roughly the weight of a German Shepherd dog.) and I was so physically weak that even the half-hour walk had become too exhausting to be a pleasure.

Having established to my reasonable satisfaction that taking the mickey did not appear to be too dangerous a sport with, I hoped, the additional virtue of doing something to damage the morale of those I could get at, I decided to extend the scope of my operations to wider fields. This called for an analysis of the mentality of the SS; an assessment of their state of mind and of their attitude to each other; where they were vulnerable; and what they were likely to fear most.

The first established fact was that while, at least at the level with which I was dealing, the Gestapo were vindictively cunning, they were not very clever and some of the rank and file SS were downright stupid. The older ones, who had joined because they were too unintelligent to earn a living any other way, were comparatively easy going unless frightened. The younger ones, who had volunteered with a zeal inspired by their brainwashing in the Hitler Youth, were no more intelligent but a great deal more dangerous. They were also ambitious for promotion and coveted the shoes of their older companions whose rise can only have been as the result of long service. Thus there was no love lost between the two age groups. Similarly there was no loyalty within the age groups themselves either.

The keynote of the SS, as explained to me by Max in Tunis, was 'camaraderie', typified by their official mode of address. Whereas a soldier addressed his officers as 'Herr Leutnant' or 'Herr Major' or whatever, the lowliest SS man addressed even the most senior of his officers without any 'Herr' at all – merely 'Standartenführer' or 'Obergruppenführer' and so on. The idea that they were all brothers in an élite corps was no doubt good in essence, but the practical result was nil. They all wore the same field-gray uniforms of shabby material and deplorable cut but the illusion of equality was spoilt by the ever increasing incrustations of silver braid, which became more vulgarly ostentatious as the wearer's rank was higher.

My investigations got off to a good start one pleasant Sunday afternoon as two elderly guards took the sun outside my cell window. They were both, it seemed, smarting under some reprimand administered by the RSM. That sort of grudge is normal in any army, but the interesting thing about this particular resentment was that they had both been threatened, not with some routine punishment, but with posting to the Russian front. It was patent from their conversation that this was the whip which kept all the subordinate ranks toeing the line – terror of the Russian front, with the rigours of winter not so very far away. And it was very certain that the RSM could carry out his threat for he was a Gestapo man.

Since at that time I was still concealing from the guards that I was learning German, they tended to speak freely between themselves within my hearing, and I occasionally heard one of them force compliance from another by threatening to 'tell the RSM' of some sin of omission or commission on the part of the reluctant party. It was plain that 'camaraderie' within the ranks of the SS was non-existent and that any one of them would have been glad to help a comrade along the road to the east on two simple principles: the fewer there were left behind, the less likely it was that they themselves would be sent and, if the victim happened to be of higher rank, there would be a chance of promotion.

For me this was all valuable ammunition.

The next problem was how to apply the knowledge gained. Baiting the Camp Kommandant was all very well, for he believed he could get his own back by the infliction of sanctions, but the ordinary SS were in a different category. They had no retaliatory powers other than a bullet in the back of one's neck while one was 'attempting to escape'. Although I was under the hostage umbrella as far as the guards were concerned, a frightened man can do things he would not otherwise have dared to undertake, particularly if this seems to be the only way to be rid of a threat.

There were plenty of precedents for guards knocking off prisoners with impunity and I could not tell how far my present status could protect me. It would be necessary to apply the treatment in such a way that the victim could, by doing what I wanted, feel that the danger to himself was averted. Also, as far as these small fry were concerned, I was not interested in mental cruelty unless there was some material benefit to myself. I know only one name for this – blackmail.

Blackmail entails possession by the blackmailer of knowledge to the disadvantage of the intended victim, the publication of which would place that victim in a position he is not prepared to face. The blackmailee must be satisfied that by meeting the blackmailer's demands he will be safe from betrayal, and the demands themselves must be such that the victim can meet them without any intolerable strain on his resources. That he is inevitably doing so on the never-never is a circumstance he can only accept.

Briefly, the problem from my point of view was: what did I know which, if revealed to the Kommandant as having come from one of the guards, would result in my nominee being sent to the Russian front, or at least cause him to fear that he would be? The answer was ready to hand as I had already proved with the wretched Schmidt in the early hours of Christmas morning.

The next thing was: for what should I blackmail the guard? I was determined to blackmail some German for something, if only to deprive him of any peace of mind he might at the time enjoy.

With the best will in the world no guard could have got me out of the camp through the controls which existed at every exit. If I asked for more food, my demand could hardly have been met without detection. It was a problem. Then the Camp Kommandant solved it by stopping my cigarette allowance.

The night after this had happened, and I had had to fall back on the emergency reserve, Schmidt was on duty. Having fallen for the gambit once, he was the obvious candidate for the next episode.

First, I gave him plenty of time to get to sleep. Then at about midnight I pressed the 'Rufen' button. I could hear the bell tolling away up the corridor and, judging by the time it took Schmidt to answer, he needed a lot of waking up. Finally, he unlocked the cell door, pressed the 'Abstellen' button to stop the noise and asked me surlily what I wanted. I had a cigarette ready and asked him for a light. Personally, if I had been in his place, I would certainly have expressed myself with some force and equally certainly refused the request in a pretty curt way. But Schmidt produced his matches and obliged. A good start.

'Thank you,' I said, 'I hope I didn't wake you up.'

'As a matter of fact, you did.'

'I'm sorry, but you too are a smoker and you know what it feels like to be unable to indulge for want of a match.'

'Well, you'll have to overcome that urge now after the Kommandant's ruling about your ration.'

'The very thing I wanted to talk to you about.'

'Why me? I can't alter the Kommandant's orders.'

'Never mind the Kommandant's ruling. Now I have to rely on you, so, when you come back on duty on Tuesday morning, please bring me two hundred cigarettes.'

There was a pause while he worked this out. Then the penny dropped.

'What?' he cried, 'If I did that I could be sent to the Russian front, or the gallows.'

'Now listen. You remember what I told you about Kokorin?'

'Yes.'

'There is also Monsieur Raymond Amar. Do you know why he was arrested?'

'No.'

'He defended the French Prime Minister Léon Blum at the Riom trial in France; and Blum is a Jew. So is Amar. Graf von Halem is here in prison also. Do you know why?'

'No.'

'He misled the Nazi authorities about the exploitation of coal in the Donetz Basin. Shall I tell you about some of the other prisoners?'

'How did you discover all this?' stammered Schmidt.

'Never mind. What would happen to you if I repeated all this to the Kommandant and said I got it all from Unterscharführer Schmidt? You remember I asked you that once before.'

Schmidt said nothing.

'I could say that you told me because you were drunk, or because you thought I would see that you were all right when Germany has lost the war.'

'Very well, mein Herr,' said Schmidt, 'I will bring the cigarettes on Tuesday.'

On Tuesday the cigarettes duly arrived and from then on I smoked as I liked.

Meanwhile the communications network was spreading. On sound I had Stetzko and Kokorin. By the written word I was in touch with Yvon Delbos, the Bishop of Lublin, Raymond Amar, Stepan Bandera, Lieutenant Commander Michael Cumberlege (who had been captured during a commando raid on a Greek island) and others, mostly Ukrainians and Poles, whose names I cannot now recall. Later certain Germans were admitted: Graf von Halem, General Alexander von Falkenhausen (who arrived later), General Franz Halder (sometime Quartermaster General) and others. One whom I constantly refused to accept, having caught sight of him once and instantly distrusted, was Doktor Hjalmar Schacht, finance expert and at one time President of the Reichsbank.

My correspondents were not regular subscribers all the time. Some came later, some left the camp, and some died. Cumberlege, for a reason I could not discover, was shot in the back of the neck one Sunday afternoon while sitting in his cell – I expect they needed the space. The Bishop of Lublin was killed towards the end of 1944, probably for the same reason.

It was alleged that Raymond Amar committed suicide but this, in the light of our lengthy correspondence, I do not believe. Raymond was full of plans for after the war and wrote frequently of all the things he was going to do when he was free again and of his wife and family. I think he too had my philosophy of subduing fear by immersing oneself in thoughts. We were going to meet during the first summer after the war at his villa in Brittany. Above all, he had a Jew's moral strength and determination to survive. He too left no trace and I have no doubt he was killed in his cell and his body thrown into the crematorium whose chimney – in full view of my cell window – smoked day and night all the time I was in Sachsenhausen.

Graf von Halem seemed to be particularly hated by the SS who lost no opportunity to try and humiliate him. He was a very big man and they issued him with the smallest blue and grey striped uniform they could find, but he never looked undignified. It is lucky that I had not met him before I embarked on my arrogant aristocrat routine for he was a charming man and no recommendation for its success. He was not a Prussian. I think the real reason for his unpopularity was that he had betrayed the Third Reich and the Gestapo, always resentful of those better born than themselves, were taking their revenge on a class of society they consistently suspected of disloyalty to Hitler and his régime. As befitted a Graf (or Count), he was eventually beheaded instead of being hanged, but in the bestial way devised by the Gestapo – his head face upward on the block so that he could see every movement and preparation of the headsman, up to the flash of the descending axe.

Karl, the barber, kept me supplied with bits of pencil for correspondents who had nothing with which to write their messages. If he had been caught the story was to be that they were for me personally and, to support this fiction, I always had a few pages of 'memoirs', written in pencil, hidden in my cell and ready as evidence.

I hoped that a corner of my hostage cloak would give some protection to Karl but fortunately the need to test it never arose for we were never detected. I also took into account that the SS appreciated Karl's tonsorial skill and, since communication between prisoners would not be suspected, he would get off with a mild rebuke.

Probably the most vulnerable link – also never detected – was the one with Raymond Amar, whose cell was in the same corridor as mine and on the same side. When the midday and evening meals were served the cell doors were opened outwards into the corridor, at right angles to the wall. In this way the prisoners, or so the guards seemed to think, could not see each other as they waited for their bowls. Actually the doors were so thick that, when open like this, there was a three-inch gap between the edge of the door and the wall, through which we could see each other all the way up the corridor. A guard patrolled up and down to make sure prisoners kept out of sight of each other while Karl and his brother Witness delivered the food.

Message passing took place at the evening meal when only one guard was on duty, and then only when that guard was Schmidt. Schmidt affected a very large 9-millimetre pistol which he carted round in a holster pushed round on his belt to the middle of his back. Sagging under the weight, this left a considerable gap between the top of the holster and Schmidt's back. If Raymond or I had a message for the other, it was folded into a long spill and waved between door and wall until the recipient had seen it and agreed to collect. The spill was then delicately inserted into the gap between holster and back as Schmidt plodded past, and as delicately removed by the addressee as the courier lumbered by in total ignorance of what was taking place. I got the idea from having seen in my childhood days the Flying Scotsman picking up and dropping mail at full speed between London and Edinburgh. Fortunately Schmidt's speed fell short of that of the Flying Scotsman. It was by horning in on this link that Graf von Halem joined the network.

A very heavy burden was soon placed on this correspondence by requests for war news. Of the whole circle of pen friends only Stetzko, Kokorin, Halem, Amar and I could hear the broadcasts from the outside loudspeaker and of these Amar and Kokorin understood no German. Then, of course, there were the others who could not hear the broadcasts anyway. Kokorin was looked after by Stetzko tapping through the wall but, as soon as the others realised that I could hear and understand the bulletins, requests for information started pouring in and assuaging this very understandable thirst started taking up altogether too much of my time and, let us face it, dwindling energy.

I therefore decided to go into the newspaper publishing business.

All my clients were advised that, starting on the following Friday, a weekly newssheet would be issued in two languages – English and French (for at that time I could not possibly have coped with German composition) – to be known as the *Oranienburg Echo* and *l'Echo d'Oranienburg*. It was only at Easter 1944 that I embarked on the German edition which I called the *Oranienbürgische Zeitung* (newspaper). I could not use the word *Echo* in the German edition for I could never discover whether the word in German was masculine, feminine or neuter and it would have been a pity to have a grammatical clanger in the very title.

The paper would be distributed in the usual way and would contain the latest war news and a gossip column.

Each issue consisted of one sheet, about six inches by three (a format dictated by the size of the 'toilet paper' margins from which it was made up), closely covered on both sides with very small writing. Being untroubled by strikes and lockouts (though actively encouraged by a permanent 'lock-in'), paper shortage, censorship or shortage of copy, I was able to go to press with unbroken regularity until I left Sachsenhausen in February 1945. I can also claim that I never lost a reader other than by forcible removal or sudden death.

No copy was ever discovered by the Gestapo or, if it was, they never discovered from where it came although by that time they might have guessed. Had they seen it, the part they would most certainly have appreciated least was the gossip column. This consisted of biographical sketches and intimate stories about our SS men, as vitriolic as they were fictitious, all so authoritatively declared that there was no apparent reason to doubt their veracity.

This thirst for news caused me to instruct Schmidt (for by this time the blackmail racket was in full swing) to pass on to me each day his copy of the *Völkischer Beobachter*, the official Nazi newspaper, and a very interesting publication it turned out to be. While it gave little essential news I had not already heard over the radio, it did help me to identify place names I had failed to grasp by ear. It also shed a good deal of light on official efforts to boost the wilting morale of the German population which by this time needed quite a lot of boosting.

One angle which caused me some amusement was the exposition of British humour as a sign of the mental feebleness – and therefore the lack of morale – of the British people. In the modern idiom it would no doubt have been described as 'sick'. While this sense of humour is not, admittedly, everybody's cup of tea, much of it was patently incomprehensible to the earnest Nazis who were trying to analyse it. This, they concluded, was indicative of a degree of mental degeneration, symbolic of every facet of the British character, which could only result in that nation's early collapse.

On one occasion I came across a representation of the famous three monkeys, lifted either from one of the London dailies or from *Punch*. In this case there were four monkeys. The first three had their hands as usual over mouth, ears and eyes and the fourth was flapping its hands with its thumbs on its temples. Each face was that of Doktor Goebbels and the captions were: 'I say no good', 'I hear no good', 'I see no good', and 'I'm up to no good'.

This was represented, with due credit to the journal from which it had been lifted, as a desperate attempt on the part of the Jewish-controlled English press to counter the enormous damage being done to the morale of the British population by the statements of the German Minister whose eloquence and logic the British warmongers most greatly feared. It was then carefully explained that this decay was fast spreading throughout the enemy population and must shortly lead to the collapse of the British war economy and the consequent impossibility of pursuing the war which had been forced on an unwilling nation by Jewish financiers, and which they only continued to wage against hopeless odds because they were dominated by the snake-like tongue of the puppet Churchill.

On another occasion they reproduced Bruce Bairnsfather's cartoon from the First World War in which Old Bill and Young Bill were sheltering in the ruins of a cottage with a very large shell hole in one wall.

Young Bill: 'Wot made that 'ole, Bill?'
Old Bill: 'Mice.'

German press comment: Old Bill did not want to destroy Young Bill's morale by admitting that the hole had not in fact been made by mice, but by a well-aimed high-power German shell.

To what extent these efforts reassured the average German citizen I was not in a position to judge.

My major editorial triumph was the 'Great Scoop'.

On the evening of 6 June 1944 the radio announced that there had been an enemy raid on the coast of France which had been easily repulsed. The British and Americans had suffered great loss of life and the situation was fully under control. The commentator added that the enemy seemed to have learned nothing from the previous disastrous raid on Dieppe.

Franz, the gardener, returned each night to the main camp where he slept. On the morning of the 7th June he lined up as usual with the other prisoners to be counted and sent off to work and, on this occasion, the Camp Adjutant attended the parade as he did from time to time. Franz heard him tell the NCO in charge of the parade that on the previous evening he had met a friend, who worked in the head office of Kaltenbrünner's *Reichssicherheitsdienst* (the Gestapo equivalent of Army Intelligence), who had told him that it was no hit-and-run raid in Normandy but a full-scale invasion. The German forces, who had been expecting the attack up round Calais, had been caught with their pants down. Half an hour later Franz was weeding the bed under my window and telling me all he had heard.

This was hot stuff.

It was blindingly obvious to all of us who had hopes of survival (and by this time there were half a dozen of us designated as hostages) that there would be no freedom until the Germans had been finally defeated. It was just possible, of course, that the Russian advance – now in full swing – could be pressed on as far as Berlin but, without a simultaneous assault on the western front, this seemed unlikely for the Russian lines of communication would be lengthening while the Germans would be retreating towards their sources of supply. Also there were many who, like Yaroslav Stetzko, had no desire to exchange their German prison for a Russian one. If this were indeed the so eagerly awaited Allied landing in the west and it was successful, then we were entering the last lap on the road to freedom.

I was in a quandary.

This was Wednesday morning and publishing day was Friday. I could easily get out a special edition which could be 'on the streets' before then – that is, delivered to all my subscribers. On the other hand, if Franz or the Adjutant had got hold of a groundless scare, the subsequent disappointment would be catastrophic for the morale of my friends for this was their only hope of survival. In the end I decided to go ahead, which I would not have done had the news come from any other source. I put out my special edition.

The Wednesday *Völkischer Beobachter* only repeated the war bulletin of the previous evening, adding a few reminiscences of the Allied losses at Dieppe, and the evening broadcast still referred to the 'raid' and thought it might be a rehearsal for the real thing 'next year'. I slept badly that night for a number of reasons. For one thing I was worried stiff that I might have started a canard which could literally so depress one or two of my readers that they would abandon hope and commit suicide. I was also on tenterhooks on my own account for I would never be free if there were no successful invasion.

Next day the *Völkischer Beobachter* still did nothing to set my mind at rest. I think waiting for the evening bulletin on the radio was one of the longest days of my life for, if it did not announce the invasion, then either it had really been only a raid or it had been an invasion which had failed. One thing which was certain was that if there had been an invasion which had been unsuccessfully repulsed, the war bulletin broadcast by the powerful *Deutschlandsender* transmitter which was listened to by all the troops in the field would have to admit it. You can keep such things from the civilian population but not from the men on the spot.

At eight o'clock that night the *Wehrmachtbericht* confirmed that the British and the Americans had established 'precarious bridgeheads' on the French coast between Caen and the Cotentin peninsula and that all necessary measures had been taken to throw them back into the sea.

I had a lot of congratulatory messages from my subscribers. Apart from the fact of the invasion itself, what seemed to have impressed them most was my naming the area in Normandy where it had taken place, for none of us had expected it to be in that region when it came. Neither it seemed had the Germans. It was only after the war that one heard of the RAF 'window' operation and of the 'man that never was'.

From then on I had only to relay the radio information which, as I have mentioned, had to be reasonably accurate, particularly with regard to the towns which had been evacuated. I altered the wording of course. If the radio said that German troops had withdrawn from Rennes to prepared defence positions according to plan, I wrote that the advancing Allies had driven the Germans out of Rennes in confusion and with heavy losses.

While on the subject of the press I should mention the speeches made by Doktor Goebbels on the radio every Thursday evening at half past seven. There can be no doubt that he was a remarkably clever man. At the end of each of his broadcasts, even after the failure of the last German counter-offensive in the Ardennes, he had me wondering if the Allies were really going to win the war. There is no question but that he was responsible, more than any other individual, for keeping the Germans fighting long after all hope of victory was lost. It was always a relief to hear the war bulletin at eight o'clock and learn that a couple more towns in the west, in the east and sometimes in Italy had been taken by the Allies.

Goebbels made great play with the German secret weapons, the *Vergeltungswaffen* (revenge weapons) of which Britain only experienced the V1 and V2. According to him there were V3 and V4 at least still to come. The V3 was a long-range gun, intended to bombard southern England, including London. V4 was a long-range rocket gun. Both were built and became partially operational.

During the summer of 1944 a crisis arose: a shortage of matches. It appeared that Germany was suffering from a severe lack of this commodity and, while Schmidt was still able to keep me in cigarettes, even he could not find matches. This was very serious but, as usual, a solution was found simply because in solitary confinement there is plenty of time to make even the most trivial problem the subject of serious study. And this problem was far from trivial.

During my perambulations in the garden, before this privilege was withdrawn, I had once found about six feet of electric flex which with the magpie instinct one acquires in prison I had hoarded. Also, at a very early date, I had loosened the screws of the cover plate of the *Rufen/Abstellen* fitting so that its workings could be investigated at leisure. Inspection – and a nasty shock – had revealed that the system operated on the 220-volt mains. Here then were the elements to hand for an electric lighter. The insulation was stripped off the flex and one strand of wire removed which, when applied across the mains, proved to be too long to get warm. I shortened it inch by inch until it glowed dull red and could light a cigarette. After cutting several other pieces of wire to exactly the same length as spare elements, the original was rolled into a coil, a short insulated piece was attached to each end for holding purposes, and the match shortage was circumvented. Of course the cover had to be taken off the bell push every time I wanted to smoke and then replaced but time was by no means of the essence. It was not long before Schmidt was coming to me when he wanted a light, but he never did find out how it was done.

It was during the summer of 1944 that an RAF officer was installed in the Zellenbau. This was at once reported to me and I lost no time getting in touch. He was Wing Commander 'Wings' Day, who had escaped so persistently from PoW camps that, with two equally footloose companions, he had been sent to Sachsenhausen for safer keeping.

It was from him that I first heard of the 'Sonderlager' (or special camp) which had been built on the edge of the camp proper. This I learned contained, among others, my old friend and colleague Peter Churchill, the Russian General Bessonov, five Greek generals, headed by Papagos, and some others. Day and his companions had also been sent to the Sonderlager but, having escaped from there too, Kaindl, who would have been in dire trouble if they had not been recaptured, clearly thought they would be safer in cells. From these there was, as I well knew after eighteen months research, no escape.

Peter Churchill had always told me that if he were caught on one of his missions to the French Resistance he would claim to be a relation of the Prime Minister. In fact he was nothing of the sort but he believed, rightly as it turned out, that it could do no harm and might do some good. It is interesting that both Peter and I tried the important family trick on the Gestapo and that, without our having any knowledge at the time of the hostage scheme, it saved both our lives.

Although Peter and his colleague Odette, who were arrested together, both steadfastly maintained this fiction and at the same time pretended that they were married, there never seems to have been any thought in the minds of the Gestapo of including Odette in the hostages. It was, however, by using this story that Odette was able in the last days of the war to persuade the Kommandant of Ravensbrück concentration camp for women to arrange her escape.

Can it be that the Nazis regarded women as of so little importance that they imputed the same attitude to the Allies? It is a fact that there were no women hostages in their own right; only Madame Blum and Frau von Schuschnigg who happened to be with their husbands and those women who had been arrested as relations of the 20th of July conspirators. I may be wrong.

The presence of Peter in the Sonderlager together with Bessonov and the Greeks was definite confirmation, if any were needed, of the hostage theory. I hoped that, particularly as they were issued with Red Cross parcels and I was not, I might be moved over to join them but it was not to be. In fact the Sonderlager was evacuated quite independently of the Zellenbau, the occupants being moved south to Flossenbürg a couple of weeks before the rest of us were shipped off to Buchenwald, and Peter and I did not come together until we were all gathered in Dachau.

Chapter 9

The Nazi Way

The tender mercies of the wicked are cruel.
Proverbs: Chapter 12, verse 10

Apart from being kept steadily occupied with correspondence and the weekly publication of the *Echo*, I made a point of finding out as much as possible about everything that went on in our small parish. For example, two or three cells on the other side of the corridor intrigued me for some time because their windows were permanently boarded up on the outside which must have made them completely dark. When, however, I was able to establish that they were only used for short sentences passed on erring SS men I lost interest.

On the other hand the cell on my right appeared to be used for short-term tenants of a different sort. They were always in civilian clothes, not in the blue and grey stripes of the prisoners out in the camp, and always disappeared within a week or two. It eventually emerged that they were all Germans who had been condemned to death for some unpatriotic activity, such as stealing ration cards or spreading alarm and despondency, and were parked in that cell until it was convenient to hang them. A few were prepared to talk round the window frames but most were either too scared or too apathetic to communicate.

The most pathetic and to my mind the most revealing of Nazi character and methods was a boy of nineteen, too consumptive to serve with the colours, who had been detected listening to the British Broadcasting Corporation. When I asked him how he had been caught he revealed that he had spoken of what he had heard to his mother and she, a paid-up Party member, had reported him to the Gestapo, no doubt feeling that the merit thus acquired outweighed the loss of a son not even fit to fight for the Fatherland. It seemed that a Party member's word was enough to justify a conviction without bothering with the formality of a trial.

To me the most dreadful aspect of the story was not that the mother had deliberately sent her son to his death for what, after all, it would be difficult to classify as a capital offence, but rather that the son in no way blamed his mother for what she had done to him. In his view she, as a good Party member, had only done her duty. The fault which was to cost him his life had been entirely his own. He should not have listened to the BBC in the first place and, having done so, he should have known better than to tell a Party member, even if she was his own mother. Such was the teaching of the Hitler Youth. A few days later he was taken out and hanged, blaming to the last not his mother but himself.

One had, of course, heard rumours of atrocities in German concentration camps even before the war and now that I was in one I felt that I should check up on this point but, secure in my cell, I was completely ignorant of what went on outside in the camp. In order to visit the doctor I feigned extreme illness, but the doctor came to me. So I acquired toothache, which worked very well, and Lux was detailed next day to take me to the dentist.

The dental surgery was at the other end of the camp from the Zellenbau, a walk of at least half a mile. The building was quite well equipped in the functional and unattractive style of dental surgeries everywhere – apparently because nearly all the clients were SS men? The thirty-odd thousand prisoners in the camp were not so pampered and I was no doubt enjoying the privilege due to a hostage.

The dentist was a Dutch prisoner who, when we knew each other better, proudly claimed that he had sabotaged more sound German teeth than he had ever had patients before the war. He had observed that contingents of young Waffen-SS were drafted into the camp for guard duties pending posting to the Russian front and, before leaving for that rugged destination, they came to him for a dental check-up. He conceived it to be his duty to do what he could to diminish their fighting efficiency.

His technique, as I understood it, was simple. Having selected the soundest molar in his victim's head, he would drill it until the nerve was substantially exposed. The yawning cavity thus created was then filled with a compound guaranteed to fall out after a very short time. His assistant, who among other things prepared this sinister mixture, was also a Dutchman sharing his chief's intense dislike for the Germans and whose courage was of an equally high order. I have not been able to discover whether these two very gallant men survived the rigours of the camp or escaped the peril in which they deliberately chose to place themselves.

When I had explained to the dentist (whose name I never knew) the reason for my visit, we agreed that the treatment should be prolonged for as long as possible in order to multiply my sorties from the Zellenbau. There was, actually, no need for him to invent anything. After more than a year of prison food my teeth were beyond hope.

We were at the height of the hot summer of 1944 and, had it not been for the smell of filth and corruption in the camp and the dreadful sights on every side, these excursions could have been very pleasant. As it was I only continued with them because I was determined to know the truth.

All the prisoners in the camp wore the regulation blue and grey striped uniforms with a striped pillbox cap, and each had a triangle on his breast indicating to which category of prisoner he belonged: red for political, green for criminal, purple for Jehovah's Witnesses, yellow for Jews, black for 'anti-social', pink for homosexual and blue for immigrant.

I suppose people who have lived in famine areas are familiar with the skeletal appearance of those who are on the verge of death from starvation. Not having had this experience I found it hard to believe that men so emaciated could still be relatively mobile. I suppose they got the same food that I did but they were required to do a long day's work on it, whereas I spent anything up to twenty-two hours a day either sitting or lying down. And they were all in the same state. If one saw the occasionally less haggard prisoner he had no doubt been only recently admitted and would soon be as gaunt as the rest – or he was one of the 'trusties', chosen from the worst criminals and earning privileges and extra food by spying on their fellow prisoners and reporting to the SS. Sachsenhausen was not a *Vernichtungslager* (extermination) camp like Auschwitz-Birkenau, so not a great many prisoners were actually killed. Death was merely a looming inevitability.

Any prisoner called by a guard had to move at the double. One day I saw two fair-haired and cherubic boys of the SS – neither could have been more than eighteen – post themselves about a hundred yards apart and take it in turn to summon a bent and crippled old man, shockingly like a bag of bones, who was sitting on the ground. Their victim set off at a tottering run which had all the horror of nightmare slow motion, falling from time to time. Three times he managed to get to his feet again but, as he reached one SS, the other called him and he had to turn and shamble back. When he fell for the fourth time it was for ever; he literally died in his tracks. The two young ornaments of the *Herrenvolk* went off together arm in arm chuckling over this exquisite sport, no doubt in search of some other preferably more lasting entertainment. I glanced at Lux but he seemed to have noticed nothing unusual.

It was the custom of German farmers to welcome Spring by spraying their fields with *Jauche*, which is simply urine – human or animal. Beneficial as this may be for the crops, it did not add to the pleasures of a drive through the German countryside in Springtime. The urine was collected on the farms – and in the concentration camps – in large open reservoirs. On another of my journeys to the dentist (it was a Sunday and there were few people about) a group of young SS men had driven two prisoners into the urine pond where they stood, waist deep in the noxious liquid. Both the victims were Jews as I could see from yellow emblems on their breasts but, superimposed and inverted on these were the red triangles denoting political prisoners. They were made to sing to their audience. Finally, bored with the entertainment, their tormentors stoned them until they drowned. My most vivid memory of that dreadful episode is that those two men, incredible as it may seem in view of the circumstances of their persecution, died with dignity.

The persecution of the Jews by the Nazis is now history. The SS did keep records, many of which survived, although not enough to provide an accurate overall total of the numbers murdered by them. The estimate of six million Jews (men, women and children) and a further seven million assorted non-Jews is probably conservative. For a great many death was to come as a relief.

Poles, Ukrainians and so on were regarded as a sub-human species which could be used for slave labour or, if unsuitable for any useful purpose, eliminated. There was no more animosity in this action than there is in a person swatting a fly. There was, of course, an incidental opportunity for sadism, of which characteristic the Nazis seemed to have had more than their fair share.

But the Jews were a different matter. It was the policy of the Gestapo and its task force, the SS, to humiliate the Jews before killing them. The thunderings of Hitler, the cunning of Goebbels, the outpourings of the mass media and not least the teachings of the Hitler Youth had all – covertly since 1923 and overtly since 1933 – declared that Germany's one supreme enemy, the direct cause and deliberate instigation of every catastrophe which had overtaken the Reich since 1918, was the international Jewish community.

To be a Jew was, automatically, to be an active, vicious and insidious enemy of the German State, a suppurating ulcer in the flesh of the whole world, to be got rid of only by total destruction. The attitude of every good Party member, of the Gestapo and the SS, of the SA and the police, was that every Jew must be killed but, before he died, he must be made to suffer for all the ills which the Jews – and therefore he – had done the Fatherland.

- It was the Jews who were responsible for the labour unrest in Germany which was one of the immediate causes of the armistice in 1918.
- International Jewish finance had brought about the post-war slump and the collapse of the Mark.
- Jews were the backbone of Communism in Russia.
- It was Jewish financial pressure which forced Britain and France to declare war on Germany in 1939 and the Americans to join them in 1941.

This was Hitler's teaching and millions of Germans believed it implicitly. For one thing, it was comforting to have a whipping boy for every disaster which had befallen their country and for which, in fact, nobody was responsible but the Germans themselves.

Jews and other prisoners were treated as if they were animals but should we treat animals as the Germans treated their captives we would find ourselves in court. They were transported for days on end in railway wagons of the sort which in France during the First World War were labelled '40 men or 8 horses', but there were not 40 but 150 in each wagon. The doors were never opened until they reached their destination anything up to a week later. There they remained jammed tightly together – men, women and children – in the heat of the Summer and the Winter cold. Those who died on the way were the more fortunate.

In the camps themselves some prisoners were shot, some were hanged, some were kicked or beaten to death and some were left to starve. Thousands, before dying, were made to dig their own mass graves. But these methods were too slow and at Treblinka and Auschwitz-Birkenau, which were designated extermination camps, a more satisfactory system for mass murder was developed. The victims, Jews and Gentiles alike, were herded naked into the gas chambers, mothers carrying their babies and fathers leading their children by the hand. The bodies were disposed of in the crematoria but first they were stripped of what jewellery they might still have and any gold in their teeth was removed. Other camps such as Dachau, Buchenwald, Neuengamme, Ravensbrück, Flossenbürg, Mauthausen and of course Sachsenhausen were called 'labour' camps but Bergen-Belsen was labelled a 'collection point'.

In one regard the Gestapo and their henchmen failed. They could humiliate, starve and kill, they could beat and torture, but they could not break down the Jewish national pride. Every Jew I saw, in Sachsenhausen, Buchenwald and Dachau (and they were always to be recognised by their yellow triangle), however emaciated and however persecuted, had a dignity which no ill treatment could diminish nor any mortification destroy. In mourning their people of that era the Jews of the world have every right to remember them with pride, for they were not defeated.

For some time now my daily exercise had been 'forgotten' and, with the return of Summer, the lack of fresh air became distressing. I therefore demanded of Ikarius, with an air of authority fortified by the secret knowledge of my hostage status, that the daily periods in the garden be resumed. They resumed next day, which only went to reinforce the hostage theory.

I at once noticed something new. As I have already explained, the garden was bounded on two sides by the north and east wings of the Zellenbau and on the other two by the compound wall topped with electrified barbed wire. Previously there had been no noise from the other side of the wall, but now there was a steady buzz of conversation in a language I did not recognise.

Schmidt swore that, having no business in that part of the camp, he had no idea what went on there. I believed him for after eleven years of Nazi rule the citizens had found that it was unwise to acquire any knowledge about what was not one's own business. It was, of course, impossible to climb up the wall and have a look, even if I had had the strength, because of the lethal wire on top but in the course of my perambulations I had once found a six-inch nail and with this I set about making a hole in the wall.

In a few days my work was completed for it was manifest that the Gestapo had been disgracefully swindled by the contractor who built the camp for them. The cement mortar between the blocks was up to standard but the concrete blocks themselves were a disgrace. There was so much sand in their composition and so little cement that they were almost friable. This, together with the fact that the blocks were hollow, made my task a great deal easier and I had little trouble in making a suitable hole which could be masked when not in use by the first lump I had removed.

The prisoners on the other side of the wall were Russian prisoners of war and, by poking a rag through the hole on the end of a stick and waving it about, I was able to attract their attention. Within two days I was in contact with a French-speaking Russian and a new line of communication was opened.

It appeared that there were about 5,000 Russian soldiers in this enclosure, all captured during the Russian Spring Offensive. Why they were here instead of in a PoW camp they did not know. They had no complaints about their treatment except that the Germans had taken their boots and there was too little food (a paucity from which we all suffered) and, although most of them had been captured in their shirt sleeves, they were warm enough in the Summer sunshine. By day they had nothing whatever to do and at night they slept, crowded like sardines, on the three-tier bunks almost touching each other in their huts.

The last weeks of their detention were not so pleasant. They had been sent to Sachsenhausen for Kaindl to dispose of, and this he set about to accomplish as soon as Winter set in. They were not murdered, for that would have been wrong .... instead life was made such that death came quickly.

Discipline was tightened up and they were paraded every morning at 7 o'clock and kept standing in their ranks until noon and again, after the mockery of a midday meal, from 2 o'clock until 5 o'clock. Any man who moved was shot while trying to escape. The winter of 1944-45 was bitterly cold. In my cell the toilet bucket froze every night into a solid block and even the electrified barbed-wire strands sometimes contracted so much that they broke, producing a fine display of sparks but never interrupting the current. But the Russian parades went on and the men in their shirtsleeves and barefoot in the frozen snow died where they stood.

Half an hour before the end of each parade the Polish children arrived with their trailer, loaded it with the dead and dying and dragged them away to the crematorium after the survivors had limped away.

It is a dreadful sidelight on Nazi logic that Kaindl, no doubt already apprehensive about the end of the war and not wanting to be accused of the mass murder of prisoners of war, did not shoot them or have them gassed in batches, as he so easily could have done. He arranged for them to die a natural death from exposure. When I left Sachsenhausen in February 1945, out of 5,000 Russian soldiers, fewer than 400 were still alive.

I have referred to the Polish children with their trailer. These were the camp cleaning squad, which we nearly always met on our sorties to the dentist. One of the four-wheeled trailers normally towed behind lorries had been fitted with a pole, as if for a pair of horses, and about thirty ropes, each with its canvas sling.

The trailer was dragged round the camp by children harnessed to the slings, the two biggest boys steering with the pole. Wherever there was rubbish – a pile of dead leaves, the odd corpse, the bodies on the gallows, or any other refuse in the wrong place – the trailer stopped alongside and the children, disentangling themselves from the tow ropes, loaded it. Dressed in the usual blue and grey striped prison uniform, they were so emaciated that it was difficult to estimate their ages, but certainly none was over twelve and the youngest cannot have been more than eight. And every child wore a red triangle to show that he was a political prisoner.

I learned from the dentist that they were all Polish children.

The Gestapo policy on arresting a family was to send the father, the mother and the children to different camps, keeping no records of the movements, with the object of destroying from the outset any hope of a possible subsequent reunion. Many people will have heard in the years following the end of the war the harrowing broadcasts from Radio Luxembourg on behalf of parents seeking news of their children and of each other, deprived of any certainty that they were still alive. This seems a suitable point at which to relate the activities of Doktor Sigmund Rascher of the Luftwaffe medical staff whom I was to meet later and get to know very well.

As a medical officer Rascher had been very worried by the high death rate from exposure among German service personnel, particularly Luftwaffe aircrews shot down into the sea. He was convinced that, were proper research possible, procedures could be developed to alleviate the effects of exposure and particularly to improve survival techniques. What he needed were guinea pigs which could be tested to destruction point and he realised that in the concentration camps they were available in thousands. His proposal to use these prisoners for his experiments was endorsed by Luftwaffe Headquarters and approved by Himmler, and

Survivors in the Epilogue and Bonhöffer

Léon Blum, Prime Minister of France three times

Captain Peter Churchill DSO, Croix de guerre
Special Operations Executive

Group Captain H M A Day, GC OBE DSO
Noted Escapee

Yvon Delbos, French Politician and Minister

General Freiherr Alexander von Falkenhausen, Pour le Mérite

Lt-Colonel John McGrath, OBE, Irish Division
Concentration Camp Survivor

Doktor Josef "Ochsensepp" Müller
Bavarian Minister of Justice

Pastor Martin Niemoeller
Prominent Leader of the German Protestant Church

General (later Field Marshal) Alexandro Papagos, GBE CV
Prime Minister of Greece

Monseigneur Gabriel Piguet
Bishop of Clermont-Ferrand, Auvergne, France

Haljmar Schacht, German Economist and Banker
President of Hitler's Reichsbank

Kurt von Schuschnigg, Chancellor of Austria 1934–1938
Emigrated to the United States

Yaroslav Stetzko, Prime Minister of Ukraine
President of Anti-Bolshevic Bloc of Nations (ABN)

Dietrich Bonhöffer, Lutheran Pastor
Anti-Nazi Dissident

Standartenführer Anton Kaindl
Camp Kommandant Sachsenhausen, later of Vorkuta Gulag

Captain Wichard von Alvensleben, Iron Cross 1st Class
Commander of the Wehrmacht troops who rescued the hostages

the Kommandant of Dachau concentration camp was instructed to give every assistance.

I will not recount in detail what happened next. It is enough to say that Rascher killed many hundreds of prisoners in ways too dreadful to describe and which only a criminal sadist could have conceived. Many died by being immersed in ice water for varying periods and then revived by various methods. The same people were used over and over again, for increasing periods of exposure – no doubt to get truly comparable results. Inevitably, in every case, the point was reached where revival was no longer possible.

Had the victims been depraved enemies of society convicted of the most vicious crimes, it is unthinkable that a case could have been made out to justify such a procedure. As it was, the victims were young men whose only crime had been to have resisted the invaders of their country, or just to have been suspected of so doing. Yet Rascher was convinced that the results of his experiments would be of great value to the medical faculties of the western world (which is possible) and that, incredibly, he himself would be welcomed with open arms into scientific circles.

Fired no doubt by the zeal of the true seeker after knowledge, Rascher seized the opportunity to investigate a side line of purely academic concern which had interested him for some time.

This was a comparative study of the relative strengths under stress of the various components (bone, muscle, tendons and so on) from which the human body is put together. If, for example, a man's arm were torn off, what broke first? Clearly the simplest way to find out was to tear off men's arms under controlled observation conditions and note the results. So that is what he did. Anaesthetics were regrettably in short supply in Germany at that time but the subjects of his experiments were, after all, only sub-human specimens – Ukrainians mostly – so this was no problem. Anaesthetics were not used.

Another field of Nazi research concerned the children of Dachau. On a parade ground in the middle of the camp there were drawn up in twos about 500 children, all little boys, their ages ranging from about five to eight. They were not particularly emaciated. In fact they looked surprisingly well nourished and they just stood, in their little blue and grey striped uniforms, with the dumb and stupid expression which comes when hope is dead. They seemed to be extraordinarily well matched in their pairs and I suddenly realised they were sets of identical twins.

Why they had been collected I could not guess. Our guard, when I asked him, pretended not to hear me and looked the other way. After the war I was to discover that they had been carefully sought throughout occupied Europe for some experiment in genetics the German scientists had in mind. This was, of course, a subject in which the Nazis were very interested, particularly when it came to prove that a man was good for extermination because his grandfather's great uncle had been a Jew. The twins were not orphans or anything like that. The SS merely took them and gave the parents no idea at all as to where their children were going, let alone why.

I have been accused of being biased against the Germans and against the Nazis in particular and of exaggerating conditions in concentration camps to strengthen my own case. I would therefore like at this point to refer to others, not British, who have also written of their experiences and who beforehand had no particular axe to grind. They are two Germans and two French; a great politician and a singer, a Roman Catholic bishop and a Frenchman who had worked as a British agent; three men and one woman.[1]

(1) Doctor Josef Müller, German lawyer and Minister of Justice *Bis zur letzten Konsequenz* – Süddeutscher Verlag, Munich, 1975

(2) Isa Vermehren, German singer *Reise durch den letzten Akt* – Wegner Verlag, Hamburg, 1947

(3) Monseigneur Gabriel Piguet, Bishop of Clermont, Frenchman *Prison et déportation* – Editions Spes, Paris, 1947

(4) Michael Hollard, Frenchman Resistance worker *The man who saved London: the story of Michel Hollard, D.S.O., Croix de Guerre* – Martelli, George (1961) – Odhams Press.

It is not to be supposed from the foregoing that all Germans were, or are, cruel and sadistic monsters. Had Britain been occupied there can be no doubt that some British subjects could have been found to repeat in that country what Germans were doing in Germany. It is unfortunately true, as post-war trials revealed, that this was the case in France, Belgium, the Netherlands, Denmark and Norway.

It is very doubtful that they could have been found in the same numbers as in Germany but it must be remembered that children are easily influenced and, when persistently taught from a very early age that certain principles such as cruelty, treachery and tale-bearing are both manly and admirable, the very great majority absorb this teaching and apply it to their subsequent lives. There can be no Hell too dreadful for those who, through the Hitler Youth and the *Bund Deutscher Mädels*, deliberately corrupted the youth of an entire nation.

Since the war I have known many Germans, kind and gentle people who hated Nazism and everything it stood for. During the war, in concentration camps and among the hostages I met good and upright Germans who strove actively to bring down a régime they had not chosen and refused to accept. Some, like Dietrich Bonhöffer, died for their cause. Others, like Josef Müller, lived to help in the creation of a nation in which, they most earnestly believed, such things could never happen again.

In 1960 a film was made of all the horrors the Nazis had perpetrated, put together from newsreels, Allied film and films from the archives of the Nazi Party and the Gestapo. This was shown throughout West Germany and its showing to all schoolchildren was compulsory. I saw it myself and I can certify that it pulled no punches and concealed nothing. The title was *Nie Wieder – Never Again*. Let us pray it will be so.

As Christmas 1944 came and went, with no Midnight Mass this time for we had no priest, conditions in the Zellenbau got steadily worse. The cold was intense and every night, in spite of the small radiator in the cell, a thermometer I borrowed from Karl dropped down to minus 20° Celsius. We had been issued with extra blankets (at least the hostages had) and with these and the blue and grey striped prison overcoat I had got from Schmidt it was possible to keep reasonably warm in bed. This was forbidden during the day but, except for the daily visits to Karl and excursions into the garden, I refused to get up and the guards were too apathetic to insist.

It was clear that supplies of all sorts were running short. Ikarius and one or two of his staff, their field-grey uniforms worn out and apparently irreplaceable, started coming on duty in their black peacetime outfits. It led me to ask Kaindl on the following Saturday if Hitler was coming to wish us a happy new year; but there was no reaction at all.

Our food, never lavish, dwindled away to almost nothing but the weighing machine in Karl's parlour indicated that at 40kgs (88lb or 6 stone 4 lb) I seemed to have hit the bottom. It took a lot of willpower to drag myself out of bed and into the Siberian conditions in the garden to seek news of the Russians.

Cigarettes had apparently disappeared from the market altogether and Schmidt was supplying me with a sort of Polish tobacco called, I think, *Mahorka*. It seems the Polish tobacco plants have no leaves, only twigs and stalks. It was smokeable, but only just, which was more than could be said for some of the alternatives Schmidt offered such as Bavarian herb tea. His protestations that nothing better than *Mahorka* was available seemed to be the truth for Ikarius and the other guards were also smoking this repellent weed, and there were notices in the newspaper warning the citizens of the Third Reich that it was dangerous to smoke dried rhubarb leaves.

The crematorium too had changed its rôle – this to my great content. Since it was situated not very far from my cell window, I was frequently sickened by the smell of burning bodies to which I never grew accustomed. I still prefer not to eat in a grill-room. Now, however, the crematorium was being used mainly for destroying the records as I was able to confirm from occasional pieces of half-charred paper which blew into the garden. Men were, of course, dying like flies in the camp of cold, starvation and disease (the SS now never needed to do any actual killing) at a far higher rate than the crematorium could have coped with on a full-time basis, but it was so cold that the corpses, neatly stacked by the Polish children, caused no offence.

There had been a short resurgence of hope on the part of the guards when the German counter-offensive was launched in the Ardennes, but they relapsed into apathy again when it was crushed.

About the beginning of February came the ultimate proof of German despair: Ikarius started calling me 'Herr Major' instead of by my cell number. After a few days of what he no doubt thought of as conciliation, he sneaked into my cell one afternoon, carefully closed the door behind him, and asked me to sign a certificate that he had always treated me kindly. It seemed by then that, whatever the reason for the hostage scheme had been (and at that time I knew nothing of the Southern Redoubt), the camp might well be overrun by the Russians before any action could be taken, in which case the Gestapo were just as likely to shoot us all in our cells out of pure spite. I therefore told Ikarius I would think about it. If the worst came to the worst, this might well be the way to save a number of lives, including my own.

Also about this time 'Wings' Day disappeared from his cell and I greatly feared that he had suffered the same fate as Michael Cumberlege. However, it subsequently turned out that he had been taken to Flossenbürg concentration camp with the occupants of the Sonderlager and we were to meet again in Dachau.

Then, one morning towards the end of February, Lux rushed into my cell and told me to be ready to leave at any moment. Yvon Delbos had been taken the previous day and was included in a different group of hostages.

A short time later a sort of Black Maria was backed up to the Zellenbau front door and I was ushered into one of its little cells, which I had to share with an enormous sack of little bits of wood. Within a few minutes Best, Kokorin, von Falkenhausen and the Heberleins (the sometime German ambassador to Madrid and his wife) had all been stuffed into the back and in a cloud of smoke and a nauseating smell we trundled out of the camp and took the road to Berlin.

Chapter 10

Sachsenhausen to Buchenwald

... in the black stinking fume thereof, nearest resembling the horrible Stygian smoke of the pit that is bottomless.
King James VI and I

Our Black Maria, which was very, very old and sadly in need of a coat of paint as well as a good deal of more technical renovation, felt as if it were mounted on wooden springs and square wheels. Under the best of conditions the curious motion it achieved would have made a deep-sea fisherman ill. It had four cells at the front and a bench along each side of the rear part, a good half of the available space being taken up with more sacks of wood for the gas generator on which the motor ran in a feeble sort of way. Pervaded as it was with fumes from a broken exhaust pipe conveniently located under a hole in the floor, it was untenable.

One advantage of its great age and neglected condition, however, was that the metal grille covering the air vent in my cell was so rusty that there was no trouble in tearing it off. This gave an opening about six inches square which did at least let in some fresh air. I was also able to see something of the passing scenery.

In my Sachsenhausen cell, some twenty kilometres north of Berlin and facing south, I had had a grandstand seat for the day and night bombing of Berlin and I knew already that the city had taken a rare pasting. Now as we entered the northern suburbs I could see something of what had actually been accomplished – the place was a shambles, and the raids were still going on. I was glad I was not a Berliner and hoped very much that our present journey was going to take us further afield than the capital. It was, therefore, disturbing that when we disembarked after a run of about an hour it was outside the Gestapo Headquarters in the Prinz Albrechtstrasse. The street itself looked pretty battered but the Gestapo building seemed to have escaped. The next time I was to see it, in July 1945, it had been practically demolished by a direct hit.

Once inside we went up to the first floor and I found myself back in the very cell I had briefly occupied nearly two years earlier. Even the soup stain was still there on the corridor wall opposite the cell door. It was almost like home, except for the feeling that it would be a great pity if after all I had put up with the RAF were to come and kill me now.

Before leaving Sachsenhausen we had each been given a slice of bread and a small piece of sausage; these I now ate on the principle of making hay while the sun shines. Then, just to keep my hand in, I started hammering on the door. To my surprise the man who opened it was a Gestapo officer with the rank of *Obersturmführer* – lieutenant. When I remarked that I was flattered to have so superior a warder he explained that he was the officer in charge of the party of which I was a member, and what did I want?

'As a hostage,' I said, 'I want an assurance that if there's an air raid I shall be taken to a shelter.'

'How do you know you're a hostage?' he asked, somewhat taken aback.

'Oh!' I replied, always ready to do my friends a bit of good, 'Kaindl told me. Was he wrong?'

'Well, as you know already there's not much point in denying it. Yes, Herr Major, you are.'

This was good hearing, and so was the 'Herr Major' touch. Things were looking up.

'So what about an air raid? And what are we messing about in Berlin for? Hostages aren't much good to anybody if they're dead.'

'If the sirens go I will personally conduct you to the shelter – we have a very good one just behind this building. As to why you are here in Berlin, the pig of a driver of the transport, which was only supposed to stop here to pick me up with my men, refused to travel except at night. He won't realise that it's a damned sight more dangerous here in Berlin than it is on the open road. He says he's afraid of being shot up by British fighters.'

'Yes, well, it's quite a dilemma, isn't it? But where are we going eventually?'

'Eventually I'm not allowed to say and I don't know which route we are to take to get there anyway. At present we go down the Autobahn to Buchenwald and wait there for further orders.'

'I must say," I remarked, 'the Gestapo Touring Bureau does take its clients to the nicest places! Is that where we all get gassed or shot, or something?'

'I assure you,' he protested, 'you will have the best available quarters and the greatest possible care will be taken of you.'

'Fine! I can't wait to see the best the Gestapo can do! When do we start?'

'As soon as it is dark – if there is no raid on.'

At that moment the sirens began to wail.

Summoning four guards the lieutenant fetched us all out of our cells and, having shared us out among his men, led us off to the shelter. I had a guard to myself, a very old man literally shaking with fright. He was in such a hurry to get under cover that if I had gone off in the opposite direction he would never even have noticed.

The shelter, like so many I was later to see in Germany, was a great block of concrete above ground level. At the time I supposed it to be something special for the Gestapo, but it turned out to be the standard design which the Germans called a 'Bunker'. Judging by the entrance the walls were at least six feet thick and the roof was presumably a good deal thicker. It would have been comforting to have known at the time how much trouble the Allied army engineers were going to have after the war trying to demolish them.

The shelter contained when we got there twenty or thirty civilians as well as about fifty men in uniform. Whether the former were passers-by or Gestapo in civilian clothes I could not tell. As it happened, I had left my striped overcoat in the cell so that there was nothing to distinguish me from the other people in the shelter whose clothes were just about as scruffy as mine were.

My elderly escort squatted down near the door in a state of numbed terror. As the bunker was at least fifty feet square I had no trouble keeping out his sight and had a lovely time. Like little girls we had been forbidden to speak to strangers and the other hostages, whose guards were also more vigilant than mine, remained together in a group. As far as I was concerned I had no intention of letting slip the first opportunity since the train journey from Naples, nearly two years earlier, of talking other than furtively to anybody except a guard.

The air raid lasted nearly two hours and during that time some pretty heavy hardware fell what seemed to be very close to the bunker, and there were occasions when the whole structure rocked.

Personally, I was too busy to worry about it, wandering happily round, accosting one citizen after another, and asking them if they still thought Germany was going to win the war.

The response was very disappointing. Possibly because of my accent, possibly because there were so many Gestapo about, all the people I spoke to were thoroughly unresponsive. Some said nothing at all in a sullen sort of way. Others muttered something about secret weapons and that the Führer would see them through, and obviously knew that they were lying in their teeth. One or two asked me my nationality, no doubt supposing me to be one of the foreign workers of which there were so many in Germany at that time – a status which my garments did nothing to belie. But when I said I was British they shrank visibly away, obviously taking me for an agent provocateur. Taken all round, it had been instructive as an opinion poll but very unsatisfactory as a *conversazione*.

When the raid was over we went back to our cells, absorbed a cup of ersatz coffee and, as soon as it was dark, climbed once more into the Black Maria.

It seemed a long time before we were out of Berlin and, as far as I could see in the blackout, the city was largely in ruins. We did a great deal of twisting and turning and twice had to go back on our tracks, presumably dodging obstructions erected by the RAF since the last time the driver had passed that way.

At last we were on the Autobahn, trundling along at a shuddering thirty miles an hour in an atmosphere of almost pure carbon monoxide. We had picked up two more companions in Berlin: General von Rabenau and a dear old gentleman called von Alvensleben who was, it seemed, President of Berlin's most snobbish club, the *Herrenklub* or 'Gentlemen's Club' – a title which only Prussians could have chosen and which sounded to me like something to do with butlers.

With these two extra clients and all the sacks of wood our vehicle, never either roomy or comfortable, was intolerably overcrowded. The officer in charge, who originally intended to travel in the back to keep an eye on us, elected to ride in front with the driver while his men followed behind us in a small and battered DKW with no roof. I like to think they suffered from the cold. We, on the other hand, were suffering from asphyxiation.

Frau Heberlein was the first to pass out and, as my cell backed on to the driver's cab, von Falkenhausen called to me through the door to try and attract the driver's attention. This I did in the usual way by hammering on the partition with a piece of wood until, no doubt assuming (understandably) that his old heap was falling apart, the driver stopped to investigate. The officer also got out and opened the door at the back to see how we were doing.

Heberlein, ably supported by the two generals, told him exactly how we were doing and drew his attention to his wife. I suggested that death by asphyxiation should be postponed until we got to Buchenwald, where it could doubtless be arranged a great deal more efficiently and with less inconvenience to all concerned. The officer, explained, when he could get a word in edgeways, that extermination was not intended.

By this time we were all out in the road while the driver, using a torch, explored the interior. When he came out again looking in the unflattering light of the moon extremely ill, he said there was a hole in the floor. He was then invited to take himself and his torch underneath the vehicle to see if there was a corresponding hole in the exhaust pipe. It emerged that there was not exactly a hole; it was just that the pipe had broken off just under the hole in the floor and from there on there was no pipe at all.

It was then suggested that the officer should sit in the back with us, where he would be very welcome, and that Frau Heberlein should ride in front with the driver but he got out of this by saying that the driver did not know the way. We finally settled for leaving my cell door open so that we could take it in turns to get some fresh air at my window. The hole in the floor was rather ineffectively bunged up with a handful of cotton waste, and back we all climbed.

This incident drew my attention to an interesting point noted for possible future reference – this was the inborn German respect for a uniform. General von Rabenau was in civilian clothes and was not in the least impressive, and it is quite likely that this induced in him a feeling of inferiority which he could not disguise. General von Falkenhausen, on the other hand, was in full uniform, red and gold trimmings and all, and his *Pour le Mérite* hanging round his neck. When he spoke to the Gestapo, which he did in a tone of curt authority, it was very noticeable that the Obersturmführer made a visible effort not to jump to it and stand to attention. The SS driver jumped like anything.

This was the more interesting since there was no love lost at all between the SS and the army proper, the SS looking on the army as effete and the army viewing the SS with disgust. The Waffen-SS was frequently used in the field to execute measures of civilian repression which the army refused to undertake.

And so the night wore on. Twice we stopped while the driver replenished his gas generator with wood, and on each occasion we got out into the blessed fresh air. By being difficult and elusive about getting in again these intervals were considerably prolonged.

My window was shared the whole time we were moving by Frau Heberlein who certainly needed it, General von Rabenau who was a very frail old man, and Alvensleben whose gasping moans were in my opinion almost entirely histrionic. The rest of us put up with the gas, now filtered to some extent by the cotton waste but still powerfully present, occasionally dragging Alvensleben away from the window when Frau Heberlein or Rabenau appeared to be in extremis.

By the time we reached Buchenwald in the first flush of dawn I personally had the finest headache I had ever had. I was in a filthy temper and the forcible expression of my opinion on Germany, German motor vehicles, the Gestapo and the Nazi régime went far, I believe, to inspire in the Oberscharführer in charge of the Buchenwald cells the attitude of rather cringing respect with which he never failed to favour me.

I had noted with interest that on arriving at Buchenwald we did not pass through the electrified fence. Instead, we pulled up outside the entrance to a barrack block – one of three forming a hollow square – and went down to the basement. This was where the cells were, obviously constructed as an afterthought in what had originally been intended to be used as storage space.

The piece of bread and the imitation coffee we were given for breakfast was no improvement on Sachsenhausen but, for once, I was not hungry. With breaks only for the midday and evening meals I slept until the following morning.

Chapter 11

Buchenwald

They seemed like old companions in adversity.
W.C. Bryant

After the relative luxury of the Zellenbau in Sachsenhausen the Buchenwald cells were a sad comedown. Here there were no refinements for VIP prisoners, no barber and not even any hot water. They had obviously been built in a great hurry, possibly by prison labour, for the work had been done carelessly and with very little skill. The walls separating the cells were made of thin concrete blocks, unpointed and unplastered, and the whole effect was of a temporary structure intended for demolition at no very distant date. The cells themselves were much larger than in Sachsenhausen and their width had clearly been dictated by the spacing of the original cellar windows, allowing one window per cell.

These windows were high up in the wall so that their bottom edges were about six inches above the level of the ground outside. They would not open at all but, being of clear glass, one merely had to stand on the chair to have an excellent view of all that went on outside, obstructed only by the window bars. The furniture consisted of a bed, a table and chair, and the usual bucket.

Between the two rows of cells there was a very wide corridor, almost a lobby, this considerable area being broken only by the well of the staircase leading to the entrance hall above. This was closed at the bottom by a grille which could only be opened from the inside. Visitors had to ring a bell and wait to be let in. At one end of the corridor were the toilet arrangements consisting of a row of washbasins, a row of WCs and two or three primitive showers.

There appeared to be only one guard for the cells, the Oberscharführer in charge, who lived, ate and slept in the cell arranged as an office. As far as I could establish during the six weeks or so that I was there he was never relieved at all except, perhaps, once or twice during the night. From what I had seen of the neighbourhood when we arrived he was probably better off in his office than outside.

Buchenwald, as the name implies, is in the middle of a beech forest and, as far as I could ascertain by cross-examining the guard, the nearest towns were Erfurt on one side and Weimar on the other – both fairly distant and neither very exciting. It also appeared that there was no transport available, public or private, because of the petrol shortage. If you wanted a night out on the town you either went on a bicycle or walked. The nearest big city was Dresden, some distance to the east.

Outside the electrified fence there were, in addition to the barracks in which we were housed, a number of unimaginative little villas built as SS married quarters, one of which contained at that time (although I did not then know it) the French ex-Prime Minister Léon Blum and his wife. When her husband was arrested Madame Blum insisted on accompanying him, for his health was far from good and, being a quiet but persistent woman in the habit of getting her own way, she succeeded. Her husband being a Jew this was a very brave act – the more so as she herself was also Jewish.

Also outside the camp proper were the ruins of a fairly large factory which had been totally destroyed by air attack. I had noticed it when we arrived and I watched out for it when we left as until then I had never seen a more effective job of destruction. It had been a small-arms ammunition factory and its elimination, I was told, had been accomplished without a single bomb falling inside the concentration camp itself.

The daily routine was simple. Each morning we went in turn to the washroom and after that we stayed for the rest of the time in our cells. There was no exercise period, presumably because there was no suitable place for it and no one available to supervise it, but the cells were quite large enough to walk about in – if one wanted to walk about. The food was not such as to create boundless energy.

Smoking was no problem because, since *Mahorka* became the only ware and was apparently sold in half-pound bags, I had accumulated from Schmidt a very considerable stock. Fortunately the electric light switch was inside the cell so I also had a source of power for my 'lighter'.

Having nothing whatever to do I naturally turned my attention to my fellow prisoners with the object of finding out who they were and whether they fitted in as hostages. I was particularly keen to find out whether they were all probable hostages, in which case it could well be that this block of cells had been specifically built as a sort of staging post. This would account for its hasty construction and also confirm that the whole hostage business was a carefully thought out plan.

My excursions to the washroom provided little information other than that, to judge by the sound of voices, some cells contained two prisoners and that the cell on my left, the door of which frequently stood open, appeared to house an SS officer who was free to come and go. At first I supposed it to be our escort commander, but then saw from a uniform hanging on the wall that the badges of rank were wrong. I determined to find out who this neighbour might be, but it took a long time.

The cell on my right also seemed to contain two prisoners. After knocking on the wall and getting quite unintelligible answers, I decided on more direct contact. My six-inch nail made very short work of the mortar between two blocks and within a day there was a convenient hole – large enough to peer through but not big enough to be obvious to a casual observer.

My neighbours, both in civilian clothes, were an elderly German called Müller and another, rather younger, called Gehre. Gehre seemed a nondescript sort of person, bewildered by his predicament but devoted to Müller, who had prevented him from committing suicide in the cell and in some degree restored his morale. This devotion was to cost Gehre his life.

Müller, on the other hand, was quite a lad. During our captivity and after the war I was to get to know him extremely well, so I cannot now be sure how much of his history I learned in Buchenwald and how much at a later date.

Josef 'Ochsensepp' Müller was a prominent Munich lawyer, a militant Catholic and a ruthless opponent of the Nazi régime. He also possessed powers of oratorical persuasion unusual even in a lawyer. When the war broke out he was a member of the German staff accredited to the Vatican, where he had very powerful friends. When he became aware of Hitler's plans to invade the Netherlands and Belgium he passed on this information to Brussels, but unfortunately it was not believed.

When the Germans occupied Belgium they found out that this information had been passed on and that it had come from the Vatican, but not who had sent it. Müller, darkly suspected of the leak, was recalled to Germany for investigation. So convincingly, however, did he protest his innocence and, indeed, his horror that any German could commit so dastardly a crime, that he was sent back to the Vatican as special investigator to discover the culprit. After a decent interval he denounced a militant Nazi he particularly disliked and the affair was closed.

Later, I think in 1943, he was nevertheless arrested at about the same time as Pastor Dietrich Bonhöffer, both suspected of anti-Nazi activity, both members of Admiral Canaris' anti-Hitler organisation, and both victims of Himmler's determination to discredit Canaris and absorb the Abwehr (German for 'defence') into his own *Reichssicherheitsdienst*. Whether Himmler suspected that Canaris was plotting against Hitler under cover of his counter-espionage organisation (as indeed he was), or whether he was merely jealous of the existence of a secret service other and more successful than his own, I do not know.

It would rather seem that the Abwehr plot against Hitler only came to light in the last months of the war for it was only then that Canaris was arrested and executed. Indeed it was only in the last weeks of the war that, after studying the Canaris diaries, the Gestapo went all out (on personal instructions from Hitler) to locate and eliminate Müller and Bonhöffer. Meanwhile both had been moved from their prison in Berlin (I think it was Tegel) to the cells in Buchenwald and the Gestapo had, for the time being, lost track of them.

It seemed to me that Müller's high Vatican connections might qualify him, in German eyes, as a hostage.

Not many days after our arrival in Buchenwald the air raid sirens sounded at about ten o'clock one morning. It was a beautiful day with a cloudless sky, soon filled with the noise of aircraft passing overhead. The view from my cell window was magnificent and exhilarating for this was the first time I had seen a really big Allied bomber force on its way to its target. The formations followed each other in an apparently never-ending procession towards the east and, before the last had gone by, the first were coming back. The target was Dresden, and the whole operation looked like an exercise for there was no anti-aircraft fire and no German fighter opposition. The Camp Kommandant told me later that no fighters could take off because there was no fuel for them.

It occurred to me that this could be an excellent opportunity to break down our isolation, so, swinging my chair with a good wristy action and plenty of follow through, I beat on the door. The Oberscharführer was there in no time.

'What the Hell are you making all that noise for?' he yelled.

'Please don't shout at me, and remember in future to address me as "Herr Major". I merely wished to attract your attention.'

'Well, what do you want?'

I looked at him pretty sternly.

'Herr Major,' he added reluctantly.

'Good. You may have noticed that there are some aeroplanes passing overhead which, I am pleased to see, are British.'

'Yes ... Herr Major.'

'My colleagues and I are, as you may or may not know, hostages. Your superiors will not be pleased if any of us are killed by a bomb, and these windows are very vulnerable. You will therefore at once open all the cell doors so that we can all move to the comparative safety of the corridor. You can join us if you like,' I added kindly.

I pushed past him into the corridor.

'Come along, hurry up and unlock the doors.'

He hesitated. Then, for a reason which emerged next day, he capitulated.

'Jawohl, Herr Major,' he said quite smartly. Then he unlocked all the other doors and invited the tenants to move into the greater safety of the corridor.

The illusion of safety away from the windows had, of course, to be kept up, so all the cell doors had to be closed again as soon as the prisoners were out, which made the corridor pretty dark. A few low-power bulbs did very little to dispel the gloom. There was, however, light enough to see that we were a very motley collection.

Frau Heberlein had recovered from her ordeal in the Black Maria and had even done something to her hair. The other lady present, a plump, blonde prostitute from Düsseldorf, had done a great deal to her hair. Falkenhausen was neat and trim as ever. Best was immaculate in the clothes the Gestapo had obligingly brought him after the invasion of the Netherlands from his flat in The Hague. Alvensleben looked as bewildered as usual. Kokorin was, as was his custom, quiet, smiling and calm.

For the first time I met the other hostages in the flesh. Müller and Gehre I already knew through our hole in the wall. I now got to know Dietrich Bonhöffer, Hermann Pünder and Doktor Rascher of the Luftwaffe. Rascher, I thought after a little conversation, would bear a good deal of further investigation. I looked for but failed to find the SS officer from the cell on my left.

It was five hours before the all clear sounded and we all spent a happy time renewing acquaintance with some and getting to know the others.

Next morning the Oberscharführer came sidling into my cell and revealed the reason for his complacency of the previous day – he wanted a certificate stating that he had shown only the most humane consideration for the prisoners in his charge.

The Gestapo and the SS seemed to be suffering from an awakening of conscience, or at least a growing awareness of the enormity of their conduct in the eyes of other people.

I said that, provided he kept up the good work and opened the cell doors for at least an hour each day, I would consider it when the time came. He pleaded that he could get into serious trouble over it but that, I pointed out to him unhelpfully, was his problem. No doors opened – no certificate. Also, since there was no radio to be heard in Buchenwald as there had been in Sachsenhausen, I wanted the newspaper every morning.

To all this he at last agreed. In the end we left Buchenwald in such a hurry that he never did get his certificate ... for all the good it would have done him.

Dietrich Bonhöffer was a man of about 35, fair-haired and chubby in spite of his long incarceration, with twinkling eyes behind the sort of gold-rimmed spectacles which seem to glitter more than most. An evangelical pastor, he had founded a new order in Germany called the Confessing Church, a mission which he had pursued with the utmost diligence, first in Germany and later in the German Church in south London. In 1939 he went to the United States but as soon as war became inevitable he believed it to be his duty to return to Germany. This decision cost him his life.

After his return he very quickly came into conflict with the Nazi authorities and was also absorbed into the resistance movement organised by Admiral Canaris under the umbrella of his Abwehr (the German high command service for espionage, counter-intelligence and sabotage during the Second World War). It was as a member of this organisation that Bonhöffer made several journeys to neutral countries and had important conversations with a number of people, among them Doctor Bell, Bishop of Chichester. But all these efforts led to nothing as far as ending the war was concerned.

Until our arrival Bonhöffer had been alone in his cell. Then, to his delight, General von Rabenau was put in with him. The general was a great amateur theologian and they enjoyed together many happy hours of theological discussion.

Bonhöffer was a charming person who always seemed to be full of joy. His faith was everything to him and through it he was at peace. Without being a saint he was certainly a saintly man and he had the same look of serene happiness in his eyes as the Jehovah's Witnesses I had known in Sachsenhausen. He was also naïve, as so many total Christians can be and, while he would not admit that he could possibly be of any interest to anyone as a hostage, he did most firmly believe (even after the horrid aftermath of the 20th July plot) that he would have a fair trial and survive to pursue his mission in a post-war Germany which would certainly need it. His presence was, I am certain, a great comfort to us all for so long as he was with us.

Bonhöffer's life and works have been admirably related in Mary Bosanquet's biography and, more recently and in a possibly more definite form, by his close friend and colleague Eberhardt Bethge.

My next visitor was Standartenführer Koch, the Camp Kommandant. A big, beefy blond with little piggy eyes, he came with his adjutant and could not have been more affable. To listen to him you would have thought we were drawing to the end of a cricket match rather than a war – a match in which I had been unlucky to be out for a pretty low score and in which Germany was heading for an honourable defeat.

He spent some time telling me how he had been the organiser of some international motorcycling event in Germany in August 1939. According to him it was entirely thanks to his endeavours that the British team had been able to get out of the country just in time not to be interned. This visit was clearly only an opening gambit.

Next day he was back without the adjutant but with his wife. Frau Koch was a big, blousy, brassy Valkyrie with a wide smile and snake's eyes and I took an instant dislike to her – in which I was not wrong. She was the lady who collected tattoo marks not, as one might suppose, drawings of them or even photographs, but genuine tattoos in the original skin, flayed from the bodies of their unfortunate owners.

It was her pretty custom to wander round the camp, particularly in the summer when the prisoners were working stripped to the waist, and note the prison number of any prisoner sporting a particularly striking or original tattoo. This she passed on to her husband, who kindly arranged for her to have her trophy, neatly removed and properly tanned by the prison doctor who, it turned out, was my neighbour in the cell next door. If it was simpler to kill the owner first, this presented of course no problem.

The smaller tattoos were turned into attractive little *objets de vertu* such as matchbox holders or wallets, the larger ones being used for shades for amusingly unusual table-lamps made from human bones – of which there was also a plentiful supply.

The dear lady was subsequently sentenced to life imprisonment by a German court, in which connection there is an interesting story I believe is true. It seems that she was being held pending trial in an American prison. There, during what was doubtless a tedious period of waiting, she sped the passing hours by dallying with one of the warders – a man, one must conclude, of curious tastes. As a result she became pregnant.

It was not, however, until she was very close to her time that an American suddenly realised that she was in an American prison requisitioned from the Germans and hence on United States territory. If, therefore, the child was born there it could claim United States nationality and, if a boy, might one day become President of the United States of America. Frau Koch was rushed into a German prison just in time and the child was born an indubitable German citizen. It was a boy.

On the third day Koch came by himself. What he wanted was ... yes, you've guessed ... a certificate of good conduct. He even proposed that he and I should set off together, with of course dear Ilse, to meet the advancing Americans.

This I turned down at once, pointing out that before we met the Americans we would have to pass through the German lines if any, and make ourselves known to some American trigger-happy outpost which was more likely to shoot first and ask questions afterwards.

I told him that his best chance of salvation lay in doing everything in his power to succour those of his prisoners who were still alive, protect them from any further persecution, and hope that this tardy repentance would be counted unto him for righteousness. In short, he should do what he could to earn certificates from prisoners in the camp for he would get none from me. This was not, of course, nearly as brave on my part as it sounds for he knew we were hostages and would not have dared to run between his chiefs' legs by letting any of us come to harm. I have related what happened to his wife. What happened to him I have no idea.

Then, as I have already remarked, there was Doktor Sigmund Rascher. I have described in Chapter 9 what this ghoul had done in Dachau.

In listening to his story it was with the greatest difficulty that, to find out as much as possible, I concealed my horror and tried to show nothing but a lively interest. Encouraged by this and remarking that some of the things he had discovered had surprised him very much, he assured me of his willingness to hand over his notes to medical organisations qualified to appreciate their true worth, without seeking any financial reward at all.

The fact was, he confessed, he was tired of research and his intention after the war was to settle down peacefully to a nice private practice somewhere in Britain or the United States. The mind boggled at the thought of one's child being treated for measles by a monster of Rascher's calibre.

It appeared that Rascher had been arrested by the Kommandant of Dachau on a trumped-up charge in some way connected with his wife – whether Rascher's or the Kommandant's I cannot now recall.

I expect that his arrest and subsequent transfer to Buchenwald were engineered by the Kommandant who, as it became ever more apparent that Germany could lose the war, was anxious to be rid of so compromising a companion.

He had quite enough to explain away as it was for although Dachau was not rated as an extermination camp, it had nevertheless made a substantial contribution to the overall massacre. It is inconceivable that even a Nazi could have imagined that Rascher could be of any value as a hostage. He simply came with us because, in the confusion of our departure, the Gestapo made sure they took the right people by simply taking the lot.

It was from Rascher that I discovered that my neighbour on my left was the camp doctor who, among his other duties, arranged for Frau Koch to have her souvenirs neatly flayed off and properly tanned and cured. He had apparently decided to sleep in a cell so that he could be found in it – ostensibly a victim of the cruel Nazis – when the Allies arrived. He even had ideas of being a hostage but this I was determined to prevent if I could.

I never ceased to marvel at the ingenuous thinking of people like Ikarius and Koch who seemed to believe that a certificate from me would be a passport to security, whatever they had done.

Or the Kommandant of Dachau who appeared to think that on the principle of 'out of sight, out of mind', once he was rid of Rascher he would be in the clear.

Or Rascher himself, convinced that he would be welcomed with open arms by Western scientists because of the knowledge, however acquired, he was prepared to make available to them.

Did they think that they could shelter behind the excuse that they had only obeyed orders from above? Or did they really consider that the millions they had done to death, under appalling conditions and with exquisite cruelty, were indeed of such inferior stock that they did not count as human? Or were they so mentally constituted or brainwashed by their Nazi upbringing in the Hitler Youth and in the Party that they simply did not realise they had done anything wrong?

I just do not know.

For another few weeks life went on in an atmosphere of tension and waiting, not the least tense being our Gestapo keepers. The daily paper I had insisted on receiving gave wildly optimistic interpretations of the situation and these I did not even bother to read. The important thing was the daily official war bulletin which had to be reasonably accurate. Northwards through Italy, eastwards from the Rhine and westwards from Poland, the Allies were closing in for the kill. The main question seemed to be whether the Americans or the Russians would be the ones to reach Buchenwald first and set us free. However, our war was not to end so easily.

On Easter Sunday we heard gunfire to the west – the Americans were attacking Erfurt. All through the day the firing went on and, at about six o'clock in the evening, the escort commander came in to tell us that we would be leaving for the south within the hour.

It was actually about eight o'clock before the cell doors were opened and we were told to go upstairs to the entrance hall. Hanging around until I was last, I had a quick look in the cell on my left and saw that the camp doctor was asleep on the bed. Having tiptoed in and pinched his ceremonial dirk as a souvenir, I gently closed and locked the door and took out the key. As soon as I was outside I threw it away as far as I could into the darkness. I like to think they had a lot of trouble getting him out.

It was now obvious that our Gestapo had lost touch with their Headquarters and had no idea who to take and who to leave behind. They solved the problem by taking us all except old Herr von Alvensleben who, for some reason I never discovered, had been taken away the day before and lodged in Weimar gaol. The prison doctor, of course, was not among those present.

Our Black Maria stood waiting for us, engine clanking and smoke rising from the gas generator with the inside once again half-full of sacks of wood. There were quite a lot more passengers than there had been on the trip from Berlin and when we were all in we were squashed like sardines. Like this, with the carbon monoxide already coming up through the floor, we lurched off into the night.

Chapter 12

The Road to Dachau

*You must never doubt that I am travelling
with gratitude and cheerfulness along the
road where I am being led.*
Dietrich Bonhöffer

With stuttering engine, groaning chassis, and the inside fast filling up with carbon monoxide, we set off. Travelling was even more uncomfortable than on the trip from Berlin for with our new companions from Buchenwald there were fourteen of us crammed into the back of the Black Maria, as well as the usual sacks of wood.

Also, with Heidi from Düsseldorf, there were now two women to suffer from the vapours instead of one. This compensated for the absence of von Alvensleben and kept our gas prone quota up to three. Moving around in the dark, crowded, pitching interior was difficult, painful and uncertain and most of us never got near the fresh air supply at all.

At about midnight, at the first refuelling stop on the edge of a wood, we put up a strong plea for the women to travel in the escort car but Stiller, our escort commander, would have none of it. There was no room, he said. Heidi remarked that she would be perfectly happy sitting on someone's knee, reasonably pointing out that in her profession that was where she was accustomed to sit anyway if there were any men around – but Stiller was adamant.

While this argument was going on I was trying very hard to puncture a tyre with my invaluable six-inch nail, but this time it let me down. It would have needed a hammer and far more noise than I thought it wise to make.

This and subsequent halts were substantially prolonged by a simple procedure involving the exigencies of nature. As we were about to embark one of us, who had previously scorned Stiller's suggestion to profit by the interlude, would suddenly feel a sudden and undeniable urge to step behind the bushes. By the time this incontinence had affected about half a dozen of us (not all at once, of course, but one after the other like auto suggestion) a good twenty minutes of additional fresh air had been enjoyed by all.

About an hour after dawn we stopped in a wide village street and, although the door was opened, we were not allowed to get out. Stiller went into the post office, presumably to telephone, for when he came out he told the driver that there was no room for us at the camp (which Rascher, the expert in such matters, said must be Flossenbürg) and that we must go on. Had he enough fuel to get to Regensburg? The driver, who must have been nearly as disgusted with his machine as we were (if for different reasons), sourly supposed that he had but doubted whether the old ruin would hold together that far. We sincerely hoped he was right.

A few miles down the road we suddenly jerked to a stop and it seemed that, fulfilling our dearest wish, the Black Maria had indeed broken down. But it was not to be. It turned out that a Gestapo car from Flossenbürg had been sent after us to check whether either Müller or Bonhöffer was in our party. Müller, who was close to the door, was collected at once, accompanied by Gehre who followed him like Mary's little lamb. So off went the Gestapo with the two of them, apparently thinking they had the two men they were after. This eased the pressure in the van, but not much.

Shortly after the next refuelling stop, when we were all very close to collapse, the Black Maria broke down at last, shuddering to a stop by the side of the road. This time Stiller let us out, probably saving our lives.

The driver complained that the steering had been getting stiffer and stiffer and that he could no longer maintain an even approximately accurate course. Instructed by Stiller to carry out the necessary repairs as quickly as possible, the driver said unhelpfully that he was not a mechanic and that it was bad enough having to drive the thing without being expected to mend it as well. So Stiller asked if one of us happened to be an engineer who could deal with this situation. This was too good a chance to miss and, although I felt extremely ill, I volunteered at once.

The cause of the trouble was obvious at the first glance: the drain plug on the steering box had become loose, all the oil had escaped and the box was seizing up. However, having been presented with a bag of tools, it seemed a pity not to use them, so I took the top off the box and admired the aged and now gently smoking contents. At this point, as I was contemplating how best to sabotage it good and proper, the driver, who had been watching suspiciously, said he had a tin of oil we could put in and went to rummage for it.

This, of course, was no good at all; with a refill of oil the thing might go on running for miles. Fortunately we were parked on the hard shoulder of the road and it was the work of a moment to scoop up a handful of grit and dump it in the box while the driver was looking for the oil. When he came back he poured the oil in and I obligingly put the cover back on, even conscientiously tightening up the drain plug. In we all climbed and off we went again.

But not for long. A few miles down the road there was a sickening lurch as we careered across on to the opposite verge and pulled up just short of the ditch. One glance at the steering box was enough. The grit had done its job and it was beyond repair.

Even Stiller could see that we would travel no further in that particular vehicle. Explaining that Regensburg was only a few kilometres away, he suggested that it would be pleasantly refreshing to walk there in the Spring sunshine. Pointing out that in our semi-asphyxiated and undernourished condition walking would be no pleasure at all, we assured him that we would be perfectly happy to wait here in that same Spring sunshine until the nearest Allied troops – probably not far away anyway – came to our rescue. In view of his own status, we added, he would probably be unwise to wait with us and he and his men were therefore at liberty to withdraw, but Stiller did not agree.

We had stopped outside a small house standing alone beside the road and while this argument was going on a woman had come down to the garden gate to see what all the disturbance was about. She was a very prim little old lady with a back like a ramrod, obviously accustomed to standing no nonsense from anybody. I put her down as a retired schoolmistress.

Unappalled by our scruffy appearance, she told Stiller that she would be happy to offer shelter to these poor people and, collecting Frau Heberlein and Heidi without more ado, she pushed the sentry out of the way and swept them into the house. Pushing the sentry a bit further we all trooped in behind her, letting von Falkenhausen go first so that his impressive uniform could lend some sort of tone to an otherwise motley crew. We settled down happily to the milk and bread which this good fairy miraculously produced, washed in her kitchen and sprawled in her chairs, and regaled her with a story which shocked her to the core.

Meanwhile Stiller, thwarted by the old lady in his attempt to place guards inside the house (she simply told them acidly to get out, and they did) had posted them round the outside instead. Then, with the driver, he set off for Regensburg on foot to look for alternative transport. I would like to think that he had his 'pleasant walk in the Spring sunshine', but he was back so quickly that I am afraid he was able to commandeer a lift.

What was much more satisfactory was that he brought back with him a fine modern motor coach with proper windows that could be opened and shut. Admittedly it had a wood generator but this was on a little trailer at the back and caused no inconvenience. On the contrary, the whole arrangement was so inefficient and the coach went so slowly – specially up the slightest incline – that we had ample leisure to lie back in our comfortable seats and admire the scenery like Sunday trippers.

Our first journey in this splendid vehicle was very short for, soon after saying good bye to the old lady, we drove through the gates of Regensburg civil prison and pulled up in the courtyard where other motor coaches were already parked against the wall. We were escorted up to the top floor where, in a very large corridor with doors all along each side, we were housed five to a cell. It was to be supposed that there were a great many criminals in Regensburg if, with so many cells, they had to pack us in so close. Stiller and his men, having handed us over to the prison warders, went out on the town and we saw them no more that day.

Some sort of food was then doled out, and very shortly afterwards there was an air raid. The target was the railway marshalling yard and, as this was only separated from the prison by a wall and our cell window looked straight down on it, we had a splendid view of some very good precision bombing. Our interest cooled considerably, however, when a large lump of metal whizzed in through the window, breaking the glass and clanging against the opposite wall. The cell door was hammered on with more than usual vigour.

The warder who opened it said that under no circumstances could he let us out into the corridor but managed to avoid being trampled underfoot as we left the cell. As the doors were not locked, but only bolted on the outside, we at once let our companions out as well and it was just like old times in Buchenwald.

The air raid went on for some time and, for something to do, I decided to investigate the other cells to see what fearful criminals were taking up so much room. This was quite easy because each door had a little hatch in it which could be opened to pass in the food without having to open up.

Peering through the first door I came to, expecting to see some sinister Fagin if not worse, what I did see was three women and two small children lying face down on the floor. I opened the door and invited them to join us in the corridor, which they did with great speed and every sign of relief to be greeted with cries of amazement by General von Rabenau. It turned out that they were old friends.

Their first act was to beg us to release their companions in the other cells which we at once did, in spite of fretful complaints from the head warder. After a couple of years with the Gestapo one was not impressed by civilians, even if they did wear a uniform, and he was brusquely invited to shut up, mind his own business and stop making a pest of himself to his betters. He retired into a corner and sulked.

There were about fifty of these new companions, all women and children and ranging in age from about six to about seventy. It emerged that they were *Sippenhäftlinge*.

'Sippe' in German means 'family' or 'strain' in both the botanical and the genealogical sense. 'Häftling' means 'prisoner'.

After the attempt on Hitler's life on the 20th July 1944 the ringleaders – Gördeler, Graf Schenck von Stauffenberg and so on – were quickly arrested and, after a travesty of a trial before a judge who called them traitors and assassins before the charges had even been read, were sentenced to death and most savagely executed.

At the same time all the members of their families who could be found – men, women and children – were arrested and held as 'Sippenhäftlinge'. It appeared that they were to be added to the collection of hostages. The Germans presumably thought that they would be of value as the relatives of those who, by attempting to save what was left of Germany, had in so doing tried to assist the Allies however indirectly.

There is no doubt that their predicament as comparatively innocent human beings in danger of extermination would have aroused compassion but they were, after all, enemies. What is more, they were Germans who had lived and worked in Germany until 1944 and had passively condoned or actively assisted Hitler's rise to power. They had supported, or at least not opposed, the Nazi régime far beyond the time when it could be pretended that Hitler's intentions were still obscure, and many of their menfolk had held high Party or military rank under his command. The brutal fact is that, with a few possible exceptions, they had supported Hitler as long as it suited their book. At the end of the war all the Germans among the hostages were interned on the Isle of Capri for screening, and some were brought to trial.

When the air raid was over we refused to go back into our cells and the warders, submitting more or less gracefully to a situation they could not control and did not understand, gave up trying and left us alone. It was late before we went to bed that night – particularly as there was only one bed for five.

We also had a great deal to talk about with our new companions. All of them were either known to Falkenhausen, Rabenau or Bonhöffer or else they had mutual friends. The non-Germans in our group were very interested to hear their stories and to draw what inferences we could.

It seemed that, although their heads of family had been convicted of the most dreadful crime in the Nazi calendar (plotting against Hitler), they themselves had been less imprisoned than interned. They had been left together in groups and they had been allowed to receive parcels from their friends. Personally, I would have hesitated to ask my friends to send me parcels under these circumstances for fear of implicating them as sympathisers but there appear to have been no such inhibitions on the part of either the prisoners or their benefactors. They had in fact been so well looked after in this way that they all looked extremely healthy and well fed and had even been able to accumulate stocks and reserves against possible bad times to come.

In spite of our own condition of near starvation, which must have been pretty obvious and certainly shocked the old schoolmistress, they did not offer to share anything with us, and we were much too proud to ask.

These Sippenhäftlinge seemed to be almost all of them members of at least the petite noblesse – all of them remarkably toffee-nosed with what they obviously looked on as the bourgeoisie in a way they might not have found necessary had their status been higher than it was.

Personally, as an officer and presumably therefore a gentleman, I was treated with a friendliness I felt little inclination to reciprocate. Heberlein, although his name was not embellished with a 'von', was socially acceptable because he was a diplomat. Rascher was clearly regarded as a bounder, and was accordingly treated. But their attitude of contempt towards Heidi, who was after all a fellow prisoner who had enjoyed a great deal less comfort than they had, was disgusting and a sad reflection on the manners and upbringing of a class which obviously considered itself to be superior to the average mortal. It was with considerable – and perhaps malicious – pleasure that I went to some trouble to show ostentatiously to Heidi all the respect due to her sex if not to her profession. In this I was joined by General von Falkenhausen, who was a gentleman in anybody's language.

My observation of the behaviour of what was presumably the governing class in Germany in earlier times, and presumably not without influence under Hitler, caused me to think once more about the problem which had long exercised my mind: in all the horrors of race extermination the Nazis had perpetrated, where had they found the people to execute their dreadful policy? So many millions had been eliminated that it could not possibly be the work of just a few. There must have been thousands who were willing to carry out the orders they were given.

I had so far assumed, inspired to some degree by my acquaintance with such specimens as Lux, Schmidt and Meyer, that those who gave the orders and those who carried them out must all have been recruited from city dregs of which, admittedly, Germany seemed to have a very high proportion. Now I was not so sure.

Serfdom and the feudal system had lasted a good deal longer in Germany than in most west European countries, even France – where it had endured until 1789 – and that is the prerogative of a nobility which has no respect for the lower classes. It was possible in German to address another person in the (familiar) second person singular or (formal) second person plural, representing a range of superiority and class distinction. From the contempt with which one addresses someone in the second person singular to the assumption that he is not quite human is only a very short step. It was dawning on me that there was a stratum of German upper class that would exterminate Poles to clear the ground with no more compunction than it would shoot foxes to preserve the game.

This theory was in some degree borne out by the little matter of Anneliese Gisevius. This pleasant girl had been arrested because her brother had been implicated in the plot against Hitler, but had prudently succeeded in moving their parents to Switzerland in case things went wrong – which they did. Fraülein Gisevius was interned with a group of other Sippenhäftlinge with whom she lived in common. Unfortunately for her she was of plebeian origin and by profession only a schoolteacher – as such she could not, of course, be accepted into the community.

It was also her misfortune that, her parents being in Switzerland and having no friends, there was nobody to send her food parcels, so she sat at one end of the table, eating what the Gestapo chose to give her while the others sat at the other end enjoying their provisions. At Christmas, a feast the Germans treat with the greatest sentimentality, Fraülein Gisevius ate her prison rations while the others made merry with the delicacies they had saved for the festive occasion. 'Goodwill towards men' did not extend to school marms.

The Sippenhäftlinge departed next morning for an unknown destination and we left after a midday meal which, for once, was satisfying if not cordon bleu because rations were delivered for everyone, including the departed Sippenhäftlinge. It is a meaningful sidelight on the lavishness of our rations that twelve of us had no difficulty in eating what had been intended for sixty.

That afternoon we had a pleasant drive through the Bavarian country-side in delightful sunshine. The trees were in bud, the daffodils were in bloom and there were few signs of war. The occasional Allied aircraft passed overhead, but the German fighters on the airfields at Deggendorf and Straubing stayed on the ground for lack of fuel. At Deggendorf we crossed the Danube and drove on into the peaceful hills of the Bavarian Forest. It was the sort of trip that in more settled times tourists pay money to enjoy.

Our destination turned out to be Schönberg, where we pulled up in the village square after the most agreeable journey I had made since 1942. Two other coaches were already parked under the trees.

We were to be housed in the first floor of the village school, which gave every indication of having been prepared in advance as a staging post – whether for hostages or for some other clients we could not tell. We were soon established in a large airy room, with big windows in two of its walls, beds all round the sides and a table and benches in the middle. There were twelve beds in the room so at least – unlike Regensburg – we had a bed each and with sheets, pillows and proper bedding very com-fortable they were too.

We quickly discovered that our new companions, the Sippenhäftlinge, were in the other three rooms on the same floor, which accounted for the coaches we had seen parked in the square, and it seemed that we were going to be a great deal more comfortable than we had been before. The rooms were even heated by a typical Bavarian wood-burning stove centrally placed to warm all the rooms on the floor and stoked from our room. Being in the middle of a forest there was no shortage of wood and we stoked lavishly, for the nights were still cold and our resistance was low.

The allocation of beds in our room was done with almost Victorian regard for the conventions. Heidi was firmly put in one corner against the wall with Frau Heberlein next to her as chaperone. She had her husband on the other side and the rest of us shared out the remaining beds with all prospects of philandering firmly thwarted.

None of us, I am certain, entertained any amorous ambitions at all, which we were in any case in no fit state to implement. The great thing was that the conventions were respected. I was at the other end of the room with Rascher determinedly in the bed next to me, and Kokorin, who had become very much attached to Bonhöffer, was beside his new friend.

After a negligible evening meal which, after our unexpected blow out at midday, raised only routine complaints, we slept undisturbed until morning.

Getting up in the morning was a long process. There was a washroom with two basins, but it took a long time for sixty of us to use them. This did not upset the breakfast routine for the simple reason that there was no breakfast – only a cup of yellowish hot water amusingly referred to by the guards as 'coffee'. It was not even sweetened.

Stiller, with most of the escort, had disappeared after our arrival, leaving only a sergeant and two men to guard us. He had probably gone in search of orders for our further disposal. The advantage of this situation was that with only two guards (one on duty and one off) the Gestapo could only watch one side of the house at a time. As we and the Sippenhäftlinge between us had windows on all four sides, we were able to open them and talk to any passer-by who was prepared to stop and chat. Quite a number of people were too nervous to do this, but one who came every morning to enquire how we did was the mayor of the village.

The food situation had become desperate, to the point where even the SS were complaining of hunger. The position was particularly bad in our room for while in prison (and unlike the Sippenhäftlinge) we had received no supplies from outside nor had I ever had a Red Cross parcel. So, unlike our neighbours, we had no reserves to fall back on either of food or of strength.

One of our company, I think it was Heberlein who was worried for his wife, did explain our predicament to our neighbours, who promised to see what they could do to help us. However, the principle of charity beginning at home appeared to prevail in the other rooms and the contribution we received was so small that it verged on the ridiculous. It would have been quite impossible to divide it into twelve parts so, by general agreement, it was shared between Frau Heberlein and Heidi. Even so, it provided them with little comfort and less sustenance.

Frau Heberlein then suggested that, if one only knew where to look and what to choose, some sort of nourishment could usually be found in the fields and hedges even thus early in the year. Most of us were quite ignorant on this subject and Heidi was essentially a city girl but Frau Heberlein and (surprisingly) Dietrich Bonhöffer appeared to be well clued up on herbal lore, so we put it to the sergeant. We proposed that we should all go for a nature ramble along the road outside the village and gather what we could.

At first he would not hear of it, saying that only Stiller could authorise such an expedition and he was away. We offered to give our parole for the duration of the exercise and pointed out to him that none of us was in any state to run away, even if there were somewhere to run to. I think it was our promise that he could share our resulting soup which finally persuaded him. He said that he and the off-duty guard could certainly not watch all of us but he would agree to our proposal so long as it was just the twelve of us.

Still resenting their ungenerous response to Heberlein's appeal we had no hesitation in abandoning the Sippenhäftlinge to their food parcels and the expedition was booked for the following morning.

Next day we set off. Frau Heberlein and Bonhöffer pointed out to us what edible herbs they could find – mostly sorrel and nettles – and we started to forage. In a surprisingly short time, considering our feeble condition, we had collected quite an impressive heap of rather revolting looking verdure but Frau Heberlein was very pleased with it. It was typical of Bonhöffer that, adding to the heap an armful of nettles which must have caused him some pain in the gathering, he remarked with his beaming smile and the usual twinkle in his eyes, 'You see, however bad things may seem to be, God can always help!'

On our return to the school a large pot of water, of which there was no shortage, was put on the stove and the sorrel and nettles were washed and stuffed into it. The sergeant produced some salt as his contribution and we sat down to wait. How delicious this brew turned out to be I am not prepared to say. We were extremely hungry, which is a proverbially good sauce. It was hot, it was salted and there was something to chew. It certainly did us no harm, and it probably did us good, morally if not physically, and it helped to pass the time.

A more substantial contribution appeared on the following day. Shocked by our condition, the mayor had appealed to his fellow citizens to do something to help us. All official food stocks had of course been requisitioned long since, but they dug into their secret stores. The result was, for us, a large pot of boiled potatoes. This was shared, naturally, with the Sippenhäftlinge but, as the distribution was made in our room, it was done fairly and there was a satisfying portion for everybody.

As far as I can recall that mayor was the only German to whom I gave a certificate declaring that he and his townsfolk had humanely and from their own dwindling supplies most generously come to the assistance of victims of the Nazi régime. I always did like Bavarians.

We discovered later that the Sippenhäftlinge also had an arrangement with the Burgermeister. Averring, no doubt quite rightly, that if the SS were the forwarding agents for the mayor's generosity the food would get no further than the SS plates, they arranged for supplies to be smuggled in after dark by the village baker, whose house had a window close enough to one of the Sippenhäftlinge rooms for the transfer to take place. They indented for all the prisoners, including us, and undertook the distribution.

But they kept it all for themselves.[1]

The next day was Low Sunday, the Sunday after Easter, and General von Rabenau begged Dietrich Bonhöffer to conduct a service for the occasion. At first he was oddly reluctant but it finally came out that he was afraid he might upset Vassili Kokorin by offending his Communist upbringing and presumably atheist convictions. Vassili, however, most earnestly begged his friend to do as he was asked and a very simple and moving service it was.

Bonhöffer opened with a prayer and then recited from memory a short passage from the Gospels. After another prayer he preached a brief sermon, very simple and earnest, on the text 'by His stripes we are healed' in which he described the comfort and security which he himself found in complete faith in the rightness of the will of God and the effectiveness of prayer. We must not, he explained, pray to God for what we want because we cannot possibly know what is best. We must only pray to God to do with us what He wishes for us, even if that leads to our destruction. That is how God is, through us, best served.

This is exactly what happened to Bonhöffer himself. Hardly was the service over when a car drew up outside in the square. A few minutes later, accompanied by the sergeant, an SS officer came into the room and told Bonhöffer to pack his things for he was to leave immediately. The Gestapo, in their frenzied search for those who collaborated with Admiral Canaris, had found out their mistake with Gehre (although not until after they had hanged him) and had caught up with Bonhöffer at last.

In the few minutes he was still with us Dietrich just had time to ask me to get in touch with his twin sister Sabine, if he himself should not survive the war. She was the wife of Gerhard Leibholz, a lecturer at Oxford, and I saw them as soon as I got back to England with the sad news of Bonhöffer's death.

Dietrich himself confidently believed that he would have a fair trial and probably get some prison sentence, which would of course be cancelled as soon as the war was over and the Allies victorious. In fact, he was taken back to Flossenbürg where, after a derisory interrogation, he was sentenced to death and brutally hanged.

Stiller returned the same evening, apparently with further orders, and told us that we would be leaving the next day.

Although we were ready in good time for our preparations were to say the least of it modest, we did not actually set out until after midday. Stiller explained that this was because there was no way of finding a meal en route. For all we got to eat by waiting we might just as well have started earlier, which would at least have occupied our minds.

The mind that most needed occupying was Rascher's – the man was in a state of complete panic. Whereas for most of us our destination was simply a matter of curiosity, Rascher was terrified that it would be Dachau. I asked him why since we had been in Buchenwald and survived he was so worried about Dachau? Then it came out.

He was convinced that his arrest and subsequent incarceration in Buchenwald had been framed by the Kommandant of Dachau to get him, Rascher, out of the way. At first intimating that it was simply a matter of intense personal incompatibility and dislike, he ended by admitting that the Kommandant's probable intention had been to remove from the Dachau scene the man who had conducted the survival experiments.

A German assessing the motives of another German, he assumed (rightly as it turned out) that the Kommandant would imagine that nothing would come out about the experiments if Rascher were not there to blow the gaff.

'So what can he do about it if you turn up again?' I asked.

'He'll kill me,' said Rascher gloomily.

'Perhaps he'll never know you're there, in all this crowd,' I suggested.

'If we do go to Dachau, that's my only hope.'

'Well, I won't give you away,' I promised, having another fate in mind for him, 'and I'll tell the others to keep it dark as well.'

He did not seem to be very much comforted and I could see no reason to feel sorry for him.

As the journey went on, Rascher, who was sitting beside me, kept his eyes glued to the signposts. We crossed the Danube again at Deggendorf, but this only meant we were heading south. At Ganache we took the Munich road but it is also the road to Innsbruck. The blow fell, as far as Rascher was concerned, at Landshut where we kept on down the Munich road. Our destination was now without question Dachau.

It was at the crossroads south of Deggendorf that our driver stopped to pick up two young Luftwaffe officers who were thumbing a lift to Munich. Stiller was not too pleased about it but by that time they were on board and it would have looked very odd to make them get out again.

Stiller's worst fears were soon realised. The officers, naturally bewildered by our quaint appearance set off by Falkenhausen's immaculate general's uniform, innocently asked who we were and, ignoring Stiller's efforts to stop us, we told them. They had full details as to who we were, where we came from, where we thought we were going, and a description of the Gestapo's activities which shook them rigid.

Although they had originally solicited a lift to Munich, when we reached Landshut they earnestly declared that to be their destination and scuttled out of the coach as if thankful to escape with their lives. Stiller sternly instructed the driver to pick up no more hitchhikers.

The rest of the journey was uneventful. The driver seemed to know his way for once and, as one filling of wood was enough for this relatively short journey, we had no pause to stretch our legs. It was as evening was falling that we turned right off the Munich road at a sign post which read 'Dachau – 13 kms', and Rascher's worst fears had come true.

Soon we were skirting the usual familiar electrified barbed-wire fence, with sentry towers at intervals and sad figures in blue and grey stripes shambling around inside. Our fleet of coaches pulled up in line outside the main gate which, like Sachsenhausen, had its legend over the top declaring it to be 'Konzentrationslager Dachau'. Here, however, the authorities had gone further and added another legend underneath:

ARBEIT MACHT FREI

To put over the entrance to a concentration camp a motto declaring that 'work sets you free' I have always held to be the most beastly, cynical pleasantry I ever came across in Germany or anywhere else. The inscription 'Abandon hope all ye who enter here!', immortalised by Dante, would have been a great deal more appropriate.

It is, of course, true that there is freedom in death and for many thousands who went in through those gates death must indeed have come as a blessed release. The crematorium to the left of the main gate was smoking evilly to prove that, in this sense at least, the inscription over the main gate was not entirely without meaning.

Inside the camp the coaches with the Sippenhäftlinge turned left while we went straight on to the Zellenbau. Within a few minutes we were safely locked up, two to a cell in quite reasonable comfort. Rascher and I were together, for I did not want at this stage to let him out of my sight in case he managed to disappear. He had been to great lengths to keep his face turned away from the guards as we came in and repeatedly asked me if I thought he had escaped detection. He was now in the last stages of abject terror but, reflecting on what he himself had done in this very camp, I could not be sorry for him.

After a meal which, without being lavish, was certainly better than anything we had had in Schönberg, the lights were turned out and we retired to bed, to sleep as much as Rascher's restless movements would allow.

Chapter 13

Dachau

ARBEIT MACHT FREI
Inscription over the entrance to
Dachau Concentration Camp

The following day started with the usual imitation coffee which concentration camps seemed to be able to produce to a very consistent standard; it was horrible. Rascher drank his sitting at the table with his back to the door, a position from which he refused to budge. He even refused to go to the washroom thus, in my opinion, inevitably drawing attention to himself. I tried to make him understand that the best way to pass in a crowd is to do exactly what everybody else does but he was too frightened to see it – or at any rate to risk it.

While in the Dachau Zellenbau we were in theory back on a 'nobody must see anybody else' basis but the guards were thoroughly demoralised and paid little attention to us. All fourteen of us in the Buchenwald contingent except Rascher were taken to the washroom together since we already knew each other and, when we were ready to return to our cells, the guard never even noticed that I had stayed behind in a corner. In this way I met the permanent inhabitants as they came along in turn.

The first to show was Stevens, the other British officer captured with Best at Venlo in 1939. Apparently he had been sent to Dachau when Best went to Sachsenhausen. Stevens was pretty bitter about the whole Venlo incident. A regular officer in the Indian Army, he had protested to no avail when he was posted to Intelligence in Europe, pointing out that while he was thoroughly experienced in this work under Indian conditions, he knew nothing at all about such matters in Europe. I gathered that he was suspicious from the start of the whole Venlo arrangement which, let us face it, was a pretty obvious trap but, because of his ignorance of the local set-up, he did not like to protest too much.

The next in was Pastor Martin Niemoeller, whom I had never met but had, of course, read about in the newspapers before the war. His criticisms of the Hitler régime from the pulpit of his Berlin church had been widely reported and his arrest, before the war and therefore when representatives of the international press were still in Germany in full force, made world headlines. It may be for this reason that he was included as a hostage.

Niemoeller was followed by another ecclesiastic, this time from the other side of the floor. This was Monsignor Johannes Neuhaüsler, Dean of Munich Roman Catholic cathedral. He too, it seemed, had been arrested for the indiscretion of his sermons, aggravated by a long standing friendship with Josef Müller. He presumably qualified as a hostage by being of interest to the Vatican – a distinction which had not saved my Sachsenhausen friend the Bishop of Lublin but he, of course, was only a Pole, so the Germans no doubt supposed that the Pope would value him no more highly than they did.

Yet another cleric followed in the person of Monseigneur Gabriel Piguet, Bishop of Clermont. Piguet was arrested by the Gestapo for harbouring priests and Jews on the run. He was sent to Germany, without trial, together with Prince Xavier of Bourbon, subjected to the most callous treatment, robbed of his cross, his episcopal ring and everything that he had, and finally removed with Xavier to the Zellenbau as hostages.

The next two came in together. They were General Sante Garibaldi and his adjutant, Colonel Davido Ferrero. Arrested while working with the Italian resistance movement, they had at first been in the camp as ordinary prisoners. In some way they had managed to steal a camera and Ferrero's most preciously guarded luggage was the films they had surreptitiously taken as a record of what really happened in a concentration camp. I have never heard whether these pictures were ever produced in evidence at any subsequent trial, but I like to think that the courage of these two men and the risks they took to get their exposures were not wasted. Garibaldi was a direct descendant of the famous Italian freedom fighter who established Victor Emmanuel on the throne of an Italy at last united into one country.

The only other prisoner I remember meeting in the washroom that morning was Prince Xavier of Bourbon who, as I have related above, was brought to Germany with Gabriel Piguet. Himself the leader of a group of the French Resistance movement, his success aroused the jealousy of the Communist Maquis operating in the same area who, to have the field to themselves, blew him to the Gestapo. When elevated to hostage status he was wearing his blue and grey striped prison uniform. Of this he was very proud, in my opinion rightly so, and even when the Americans offered us all complete new outfits he insisted on returning to France in clothes which, by their very origin, had acquired a dignity which no military uniform could confer.

There may have been others – there probably were – but, as we were soon to be joined by a large contingent from Flossenbürg, I cannot now recall which of my eventual companions were in the Dachau Zellenbau and which joined us later.

After my return from the washroom under the eye of a scandalised guard to whom I had revealed myself when it was clear that no more visitors were coming, the rest of the morning passed slowly and tediously. An occasional Allied aircraft flew over, casually and unopposed, one being a Spitfire which crossed the camp very low and slowly, gently waggling its wings. The electrified fence and one goon tower were visible from the cell window and I suspect that a previous Spitfire must at some time have amused itself shooting up the perimeter. In any case, it was pleasant to see all the sentries in the tower scuttling down to cover when this machine came in sight.

At about half past twelve the midday meal arrived. In these cells there was a hatch about fifteen inches square in the door, which could be opened from the outside and through which the food was passed. When our turn came I went myself to collect the bowls for Rascher was still terrified of showing his face. As soon as I arrived, instead of passing the food, the SS man stooped down so that he could see my face. When he recognised me he cried:

'Not you, the other one.'

'That's all right,' I said, 'give it to me. The other one's not feeling very well.'

'No,' insisted the guard, 'you must each fetch your own.'

I had no alternative but to step aside and, with the greatest reluctance, Rascher went up to the door, approaching it from the side and trying to hide his face. But the Kommandant already knew he was there. Perhaps an SS man had seen him and reported, or perhaps Stiller had told. As Rascher came up to the door the guard fired two shots from his Lüger into his stomach and the hatch was slammed shut.

The impact of the heavy bullets at so short a range threw Rascher several feet back across the cell and he lay spreadeagled on the floor. There was plainly nothing I could do for him and, in the end, I think he was lucky. To be shot in the stomach is not the most agreeable way to die but one of the bullets must have hit his spine for he never regained consciousness and died quite quickly. I think my diagnosis was probably correct for I spent some time searching the cell but I could only find one spent bullet.

I quite expected the guard to return with my lunch – for which I felt little desire – or, more probably, to liquidate the only witness to a cold-blooded murder but I was left undisturbed with the rather messy corpse until late in the afternoon.

As the shadows were beginning to lengthen Stiller came to the cell block and opened the doors according to a list he had in his hand. Not all the cells were opened, so presumably he had either been in touch with higher authority or the Kommandant was better organised than his opposite number in Buchenwald. It was good to see that this applied only to the Dachau contingent for all the Buchenwald group was let out, including Heidi. When Stiller came to my cell I asked him if we would be taking Rascher with us because, if so, we would need a stretcher, but he just said no, and never even glanced at the body on the floor or lifted the handkerchief with which I had covered the face. He clearly knew all about it already.

As soon as we were all outside we set off on foot, accompanied by Stiller and his men, across the camp. There were the usual creeping skeletons in blue and grey stripes and the occasional more robust figure of a trusty, but the camp as a whole was very quiet and there was a hushed air of expectation.

Expectation of what? The guards were already, no doubt, fingering their false identity papers and weighing up their chances of submerging into the civilian population but for the prisoners there seemed little hope left, for dead men tell no tales and the Germans had much to conceal.

After a short distance we turned into a building marked surprisingly 'Lagerbordello'. It appeared that the Gestapo believed in providing some degree of relaxation and even pleasure for more favoured prisoners, such as informers and the trusties who, for these and other privileges, were ready to assist their gaolers in the oppression of their fellow victims. The camp brothel was one of these delights.

Who the women were who peopled this tawdry Nirvana we were not to discover for when we got there the building had been cleared of its *houris* and prepared for the reception of the hostages. The Sippenhäftlinge had already spent the night there. Our ribald enquiries of the younger and more prepossessing of these ladies as to how they felt in this unusual environment were very sourly received.

There was a large central hall with chairs and small tables, where presumably the amorous preliminaries had taken place and, along each side, a row of small rooms for the more intimate episodes. Understandably each of these rooms had only one bed but shortly after our arrival a working party brought a lot more – enough for all of us with some to spare. At the back of the building there were splendid toilet arrangements.

The resentment of the Sippenhäftlinge at being housed in a brothel was surprisingly keen. Why I cannot imagine, for the place was no longer functioning in its intended rôle, nor were the ladies expected to exercise the profession for which it had been designed. Perhaps in their Teutonic way, they were still brooding over our flippancies of the day before, or perhaps it was just offended dignity.

Whatever the reason, there was a solemn meeting of our German colleagues which ended with an announcement that the building was to be exorcised, but of which particular spirit was not specified. Pan, perhaps?

It can hardly have been Cupid. A solemn joint ceremony was conducted by Niemoeller and Neuhaüsler, apparently on the principle that whatever evil might elude the Lutheran church would be nobbled by the Catholic attack. Monseigneur Piguet looked on with a benign smile and crossed himself at the appropriate moments.

The same afternoon our numbers suddenly increased considerably when we were joined by a substantial contingent from Flossenbürg.

Our first happy surprise was to see 'Ochsensepp' Müller among them. His story was remarkable. On learning that Müller and Bonhöffer had been members of the Canaris côterie, Hitler had personally given orders that both were to be located and eliminated at all costs. I have already told something of the chase which followed with Müller snatched from us near Flossenbürg (when Gehre insisted on going with him) and Bonhöffer taken away from Schönberg.

Gehre was hanged at once, for the Gestapo thought he was Bonhöffer. When they found out their mistake they investigated Müller more carefully and then waited for an officer from Berlin who knew him personally. When the real Bonhöffer arrived, after a cursory interrogation, he was hanged without more ado. Finally Müller was identified beyond doubt and he too was sent off to the hangman.

When, however, they were face to face Müller harangued the executioner so convincingly, depicting with such eloquence the dreadful fate awaiting anybody in any way involved in the murder of a personal friend of the Pope, that the man refused to do his duty and took Müller back to his cell.

Whether the Gestapo knew this and felt that Hitler's anger was by now less to be feared than the wrath to come, or whether they thought him dead, nobody knew. The most likely answer is that the Gestapo did not know 'Ochsensepp' was still alive. Then, when the order arrived to move the hostages with all haste, they probably did as at Buchenwald and just took the lot.

There were other old friends. My SOE colleague Peter Churchill was there, and so was 'Wings' Day whom I had last seen in Sachsenhausen.

Of Peter I knew nothing except that he had been arrested in France with his fellow worker 'Odette' and then transferred to the Sachsenhausen Sonderlager.

When Day disappeared from the Zellenbau in Sachsenhausen I had feared that he had been liquidated like Michael Cumberlege and it was a great pleasure to see him still alive. With him were two other persistent RAF escapers from PoW camps, 'Jimmy' James and Sidney Dowse.

Kokorin was happy to find a fellow Russian, General Bessonov.

There were five Greek generals in uniform, led by Alexander Papagos, later to be Prime Minister of Greece. These chaps were a tough lot. Papagos was a very cultured man who spoke perfect French but the other four, while undoubtedly excellent officers, would have looked very well as the bodyguard of, say, Al Capone, or as chuckers out in a particularly tough speakeasy. One of them had more hair on his chest than I have ever seen, before or since, on a human torso.

I now met for the first time Colonel Jack Churchill, the commando officer who had successfully promoted the use of bows and arrows for silent killing. He had been captured on an island off the Yugoslavian coast and was of course a hostage because of his name although, like Peter, he was no relation at all.

Another remarkable character was Colonel John McGrath of Dublin, who had been taken prisoner at Dunkirk while serving with the Royal Artillery. After Hitler's plans for the invasion of Britain in 1940 had failed to materialise, some German genius remembered the traditional troubles between Britain and Ireland, that Ireland was now a neutral sovereign state, and concluded that there was no reason to suppose that the Irish soldiers now in PoW camps in Germany entertained any feeling of loyalty towards England or affection for their regiments. He may have recalled the case of Sir Roger Casement in the First World War, although that gentleman's experiences in the service of the Kaiser were hardly an encouraging precedent. Perhaps he thought that Ireland's independence would make the difference. He also reckoned without John McGrath.

It was decided to collect the Irish prisoners of war in a special camp and McGrath was installed as senior officer. The first idea was to form an Irish division in the same way that the SS had already formed combat divisions from what volunteers they could find in occupied countries, such as the SS division *Wallonien* recruited in the Low Countries. McGrath was highly co-operative but somehow the division just never got off the ground. McGrath always managed to arrange for some hitch to crop up at the right time.

It was then decided (and, though the Germans did not realise it, the idea was put into their heads by McGrath) to collect the cream of the Irish into a special unit with the indispensable colonel in command. Its members would be trained as saboteurs, supplied with the necessary equipment and either parachuted into Britain or landed from a submarine to carry out specific missions. This plan enjoyed the enthusiastic support of the Irish, who looked on it as a simple and trouble-free way of getting back to their units at the expense of the Germans.

At first all went well. I believe two or three men did actually return to England thanks to the efficient German organisation, handed over their equipment to the nearest police station and returned triumphantly to their units. So pleased were the Germans (for the British authorities were leaking reports of the apparent success of these missions) that the unit enjoyed extraordinary privileges including relative freedom of movement, special pay and rations and a supply of seemingly spontaneous girlfriends. The girlfriends were to prove its undoing.

A certain Irishman was scheduled to sabotage a British factory on which, as it happened, he had worked as a labourer when it was being built. Complete with explosives and £15,000 in sterling, he was sent to Norway from where he was to fly to his destination and drop by parachute. However, before leaving Germany he had confided to a friend that he planned to bury £10,000 for his own use when the war was over and hand the remainder, with his explosives and so on, to the police before rejoining his regiment. This, he felt, was a reasonable division of the money and would give him something to look forward to.

Unfortunately, once in Norway his departure was delayed by bad weather and, during this time, his confidant got drunk and told his girlfriend the screamingly funny joke about the swindling of two governments at once. Next morning, smartly changing hats, the lady rushed off in her other and more respectable rôle to report this conversation to her German masters. A hasty telephone call to the Luftwaffe in Norway brought apologies for the delay and an assurance that the saboteur would be dropped at the very first break in the weather. They were curtly informed that the mission was cancelled and told that the man and his baggage were to be returned forthwith and under close escort to Germany. So ended the Irish-German war effort.

The dissident Irish had, thanks to McGrath's honeyed tongue, enjoyed a considerable degree of comfort for quite some time, the Germans had spent a lot of money on them and had only succeeded in looking foolish. It is understandable that McGrath was not returned to a PoW camp, complete with the story of how he had fooled the Germans. It is less clear why he was a hostage.

Also in this group were Monsieur and Madame Léon Blum, of whom I have already written in Chapter 11, and they told me something of the time they had spent in Buchenwald.

Housed in one of the married quarters in the barracks area outside the camp proper, they had lived through the air attack on the ammunition factory. The attacking force had been to great pains not to drop any bombs inside the electric fence but had naturally gone to no such trouble as far as the barracks were concerned so the house the Blums were in was rocked several times by near misses. Léon Blum, who was suffering badly at that time from sciatica, was practically bedridden so they had been unable to shelter even on the ground floor.

Another house in which Princess Mafalda of Savoy (the wife of Prince Philip of Hesse) was a prisoner suffered a direct hit and the princess was killed.

Another companion we acquired at this time, though whether from Dachau or Flossenbürg I cannot remember, was not in the international class at all – he was a German circus clown. He was a delightful little man with a sad and wizened clown's face and even the Sippenhäftlinge were nice to him. For some reason or other he was always called 'Kohlenklau'. This was the name of a character invented in Germany during the war and appearing on posters to personify deliberate (or at least avoidable) waste of important materials such as, obviously, coal. He was everywhere, in newspapers and on hoardings, always accompanied by some telling slogan. Why our clown should have enjoyed this inapposite nickname was a mystery. Perhaps he started it himself.

It appeared that Kohlenklau had been arrested for repeating in his patter a quip he had first heard in a live broadcast by Willi Schäffer from his 'Kabarett der Komiker' in Berlin. Had Schäffer's consequent arrest also been broadcast, poor Kohlenklau would probably have kept out of trouble. Even so, the silly simpleton might have realised that with that particular joke he was sticking his neck out a great deal further than was, to say the least, wise.

Willi Schäffer had remarked in the course of his act that things were changing in Germany. Where it had been customary to say 'die Lügen haben kurze Beine' (lies have short legs – in other words they are quickly found out), it was now more appropriate to say 'der Lügner hat ein kurzes Bein' (the liar has a short leg). Goebbels, who happened to be in the audience and was always very self-conscious about his limp, was not amused. Willi Schäffer got no further that night than his dressing room where a couple of unfriendly SS men were already waiting for him.

This was towards the end of the war, and I have often thought that Schäffer got himself arrested on purpose. In any event, as a means of self-protection (if that is what it was) it was a great success. As a 'victim of the Nazi régime' Schäffer had no difficulty in getting permission to re-open his cabaret after the war and made a packet out of the Allied garrisons.

I have no idea what happened to Kohlenklau but I would very much have liked to meet him again. It would have been nice to think of him happily back in a circus, making the children laugh and free to say what he liked.

There was a young Belgian pilot called van Wymeersch, also I think an inveterate escaper in the 'Wings' Day class, who formed an immediate attachment with Heidi. They took over one of the small rooms and, until we left Dachau, appeared only at mealtimes.

There were others. Colonel Franz Liedig was a senior German staff officer who had been involved in the 20th July plot although, if that had been the reason for his arrest, he would surely not still have been alive.

Freiherr Fabian von Schlabrendorf had been on Hitler's Headquarters staff responsible, I think, for keeping the war diary. He had actually succeeded on one occasion in smuggling a bomb on board the Führer's personal aircraft but unfortunately it failed to go off. He too, to have survived, must have been arrested for some other reason than collaboration with Admiral Canaris. It was also not clear why he was a hostage. The only ground I know of, and a tenuous one at that, is that his grandfather was Queen Victoria's private secretary.

The reunion with Peter Churchill was a pleasure in many ways. Apart from the fact that we had been very good friends before and the surprise of meeting again so unexpectedly, both my health and my appearance were to benefit. Those who had been in the Sonderlager at Sachsenhausen had been treated in some ways as prisoners of war, at least to the extent of receiving Red Cross parcels and not being in solitary confinement. As a result they had been able to make some food economies and build up a small emergency stock which, shocked by my emaciated appearance, Peter insisted on me sharing. This was more than welcome.

The other thing to benefit was my wardrobe. When caught I had been wearing an RAF shirt with the collar attached and the labels taken out, a pair of grey flannel trousers, a short and scruffy leather jacket and a pair of shoes I had had made to measure in Lisbon for twenty-five shillings.

The shirt was now a remarkable sight. As various areas wore out I had borrowed scissors, needle and cotton from Karl and done what I could, but the shirt itself had to provide the material for patches. First the long sleeves became short sleeves and finally the tails were sacrificed, so that it finished up looking like a patchwork summer blouse. When I got home my wife was much impressed by my handiwork but, in spite of the care I had taken, the quality was not such as to lead her to suggest that in future I could look after my clothes myself.

The trousers had stood up pretty well to two and a quarter years of inactivity and I had become very fond of them so when Peter offered me a khaki battledress I only accepted the top half.

The shoes, in spite of so long without any polish or care, were a credit to Portuguese leather and workmanship. I was still wearing them on and off until in India in 1957 I gave them to the sweeper.

As I was now looking vaguely martial again, at least as far as the top half of me was concerned, I felt the urge to put up badges of rank as well and here again I was lucky. As a prisoner of war John McGrath had from time to time received parcels containing among other things replacement items of uniform, and on one occasion he had been sent by mistake an RAF wing commander's tunic instead of a Gunner colonel's. I tried on the tunic, but John was a very big man which I am not and it was hopeless. However, it did have the officer's stripes on it and it was Madame Blum who made a very neat job of making me once more into a Squadron Leader.

There was a certain practical advantage in this, apart from pandering to my vanity, for it would be a worse crime for the Gestapo to liquidate an officer in uniform than the nondescript civilian I was before. At least it would be a good talking point if the time should come.

On the following day we left Dachau for, as usual, an unknown destination. We were now quite an impressive convoy of motor coaches with, in addition, a big army truck for all the Gestapo and SS men we had by now collected as well as their luggage. There were a few SS men in each coach, but most of them were on the truck for there were now fifty-one of them altogether.

Stiller was still in command but he now had an assistant, a man called Bader, junior to him in rank and an obvious killer. We soon discovered that there were strict orders that we were not to fall into Allied hands alive. Were our rescue to appear imminent, Bader would be responsible for liquidating us all.

Most of the guards were a typically stupid and brutal-looking lot. One, a fat, piggy-eyed moron with smelly feet, attracted my attention by his invariable insolence to Falkenhausen. When I asked him why this was, he told me that he had been with the SS in Brussels when Falkenhausen was Military Governor there and, in his decadent way, would not allow even the Gestapo to kill prisoners without a trial. This intolerable interference had lasted until Falkenhausen's arrest on suspicion of sympathising with the 20 July plot.

Before getting clear of Dachau we were to see one more example of a Nazi tidying up the mess he had made on behalf of his Führer.

Presumably to avoid unpleasant accusations, the Kommandant had decided that the more moribund of his guests had better disappear, on the principle so dear to the German heart that out of sight is out of mind. The stronger prisoners had been made to dig a mass grave a short distance from the camp. We drove past a column, hundreds of yards long, of prisoners in an appalling state of emaciation and disease, dragging themselves along and helping each other as they could towards an end which one hopes they did not foresee but which for many must have been a swift release from the utter misery and incurable condition to which they had been brought by the Herrenvolk.

Our road led us through Munich, which had been most faithfully dealt with by the Allied air forces. After the procession we had just seen outside Dachau this only aroused, at least as far as I was concerned, a feeling of deep satisfaction. From there we drove south east through a smiling Spring countryside untouched by war to Rosenheim, and then south-west through Kufstein to Innsbruck, avoiding the direct route to the Brenner Pass which was, no doubt, jammed with traffic to and from (but mainly from) the Italian front.

Just before reaching Innsbruck we turned into a very small concentration camp of a primitive sort called Reichenau. The barbed-wire fence was not even electrified. Here we were allotted huts with two-tier bunks and after the usual derisory meal retired for the night.

Chapter 14

Innsbruck to the Southern Redoubt

'Is there any incident to which you would wish to draw my attention?'
'To the curious incident of the dog in the night-time.'
'The dog did nothing in the night-time.'
'That was the curious incident,' remarked Sherlock Holmes.
Arthur Conan Doyle

The following morning passed in discussion about the prospects for the immediate future and in inspecting our new surroundings.

Our present circumstances were something new for all of us. The camp had been evacuated before our arrival – not that there appeared to have been much to evacuate – and we were free to wander where we liked within the perimeter.

As a concentration camp it was not what we had been accustomed to: no cells, no crematorium, no gas chamber and the fence was not even electrified. Bader hopefully said that it was, but there were no insulators and I found several places where the wire had been earthed, presumably against lightning strikes, so he lied in his teeth.

Peter Churchill and I spent a lot of time sitting on the bench outside the guardroom at the gate, enjoying the sunshine. We were told once or twice that this was forbidden and to go back to our hut, but such orders were ignored and any repetition received with so haughty and contemptuous a look that the local guards, already considerably demoralised, gave up trying.

There were now two distinct sets of guards in the camp: Stiller and Bader with their cohort, and the resident team.

The latter when we arrived were about twenty strong but, having nothing to guard, they were steadily drifting away. Every now and then a rather shamefaced figure would go shambling out of the gate in crumpled civilian clothes and carrying a suitcase. The clothes looked as if they had been laid away since the beginning of the war and only now brought to light again. In most cases the owners had also put on weight in the intervening period and the general effect had nothing of Savile Row about it.

Each absconder as he sidled out enjoyed the benefit of our comments and advice. One elderly man, whose papers in my humorous way I had peremptorily demanded to see, shook me a good deal by actually producing them. He had a lovely brand-new identity card declaring him to be a civilian tradesman of some sort, so clean and unsullied that it was patent to the meanest intelligence that it had only just been issued. Nobody looking for SS men on the run would have been deceived for an instant.

However, it seemed a pity to spoil his pleasure in this treasured possession by pointing out its shortcomings. Besides, he might have done something to make it look older if his attention had been drawn to a detail he was too stupid to have seen for himself. I also checked in the usual way to see if it was a false name by waiting until he was a few yards away and then saying the name on the identity card loud enough for him to be sure to hear. It never rang a bell with him at all and he did not even look round, as he most certainly would have if I had called his real name.

A great many SS men, Party officials and others on the run after the war were picked up in this simple way, including Kaindl (the Kommandant of Sachsenhausen) whom I had the pleasure of identifying in Paderborn in July 1945. Their fears calmed by passing through a checkpoint apparently without arousing suspicion, calling the name on the card seldom produced the reaction which the suspect's real name would have provoked. From then on, it was usually easy to trip them up for they had rarely taken the trouble to prepare a proper cover story to match the new identity, nor been to any pains to learn it by heart. The same questions on trivial details asked on several different occasions almost always produced contradictions. It is actually very difficult to avoid being caught out on a cover story.

It was at Innsbruck that Stiller finally took us into his confidence and revealed the programme which had been prepared for us. First, he confirmed that we were hostages, then he explained about the Puster Tal. It was now that I heard for the first time of the Southern Redoubt and its establishment in this valley of the Tyrol. The final query in my mind – how the hostages were actually to be used – was thus cleared up.

Stiller explained that we could not leave yet for two reasons: we were waiting for the arrival of the last of our group of hostages, and he had to find some diesel-engined vehicles to replace our gas-driven ones which could not climb the 4,500 feet to the summit of the Brenner Pass. He expected the other prisoners that afternoon, but how long it would take to find the substitute coaches he did not know. He could only say he would do everything he could, hoping to be over the pass before the Allied air forces had destroyed it completely.

As far as we were concerned it seemed to be of little importance whether we were liberated in Austria or the Tyrol, so long as we could stymie Bader's orders. As it turned out, it was probably the move to the Puster Tal which made it possible for us to get rid of Bader before he could do any harm.

The last party of hostages did indeed arrive that day. The first I met was Prince Philip of Hesse, an amiable man who spoke perfect English. I had the disagreeable task of breaking to him the news that his wife, Princess Mafalda of Savoy, had been killed during an air raid on Buchenwald. The Gestapo had not bothered to tell him and he had hoped to find her with us, possibly with the Sippenhäftlinge.

His distress may have been accentuated by the fact that his wife's death was nobody's fault but his own. Princess Mafalda had, before the Italian capitulation, found sanctuary in the Vatican. Philip had got in touch with her there and exhorted her to come back to Germany, saying that this was essential for their children's sake. As soon as she entered Germany she was arrested by the Gestapo and confined in Buchenwald.

Prince Philip had strung along with the Nazis, he told me, because he took very seriously his duty to his people. Indeed, he much preferred to be addressed by his older title of *Landgraf* rather than the more new-fangled 'Prince'. It was, therefore, to be able to work more actively for the interests of his people of Hesse that he joined the National Socialist Party and accepted the rank and duties of Gauleiter. How much this was naïve sincerity and how much hopeful running with the pack I was unable to judge. In the end, however, things under the Nazi régime went beyond the point to which he was prepared to go. He dug his toes in and was arrested. Whether Princess Mafalda was arrested as his wife, or as hostage from the House of Savoy, never emerged. Philip himself was no doubt chosen because he was some sort of cousin of the British Royal Family.

There was also a Prince Friedrich Leopold of Prussia, but the two representatives of German royalty seemed to have little in common and appeared to avoid each other as much as possible. Prince Xavier of Bourbon had still less in common with either of them and the only time I ever saw all three together was when a romantic American press photographer tried to get a picture of them in a group in which, for some obscure reason, I was included. However, his camera would not work so this momentous souvenir of me surrounded by three very uncrowned heads was denied to posterity.

We were also joined by the Austrian ex-Chancellor Kurt von Schuschnigg, who was *en famille*. Arrested at the time of the Anschluss, when Germany absorbed Austria, his wife Vera – like Madame Blum – had insisted on accompanying her husband into captivity to look after him, and it was while they were in prison that their daughter was born. They had been reasonably well treated and the child Maria-Dolores, aged about five, was in good health if a bit thin. But it was a sobering thought that for the whole of her five years of life the only world she had known was one of guards and barbed wire, and she had never chased butterflies in a meadow.

Schuschnigg was accompanied by Doktor Richard Schmidz, Mayor of Vienna, who had been arrested at the same time.

Nearly all the other new arrivals were Germans, all of them men except for Frau Thyssen who was with her husband, the steel king. I doubt if they were hostages and I suspect that Thyssen had used his enormous influence to fiddle it so that they were attached to the party to be on the healthy side of the barbed wire when the war came to an end. He had, of course, been one of the first German industrialists to take advantage of slave labour to make even greater profits and his conscience can hardly have been clear. He had plenty of money salted away in South America, and that is where he eventually died some years after the war. They were a dreary couple, forever grumbling.

The food, as usual, was terrible but I now had the benefit of the stocks saved up by my Flossenbürg friends, who were a great deal more generous than the Sippenhäftlinge had been. Access to Red Cross parcels had another and unexpected advantage.

Bader had assumed responsibility for guarding us while we were still in this camp and it was he who, while making no effort to stop the local guards from disappearing, did insist on one of them staying on – the dog handler. The camp boasted a magnificent if rather thin Alsatian dog, who ran loose in the camp at night and was trained to attack with silent ferocity anybody who approached the perimeter fence in the darkness. Bader was at great pains to draw our attention to the presence of this fearful hound, emphasising that he could accept no responsibility if any of us wandered from the huts at night and were savaged by the raving monster. He particularly advised parents to keep a close eye on their children.

Innsbruck is at quite a respectable altitude, it was only the end of April, and we were surrounded by snow-capped mountains. There were stoves in the huts but no fuel and the first two nights I just could not get warm. Two thin blankets are not much protection, particularly when one is half-starved and I had always been susceptible to cold. After the second miserable night I decided that something would have to be done about it. At first I thought of a hot water bottle, but there were no bottles and no hot water. I thought of my mother in law's specific of a hot brick but, while there were bricks, there was no way of heating them. In any case neither would have stayed hot very long. What I needed was some source of self-generated heat and at first I was stumped. Then I thought of the dog.

I am very fond of dogs and seldom have any trouble with them so it seemed worthwhile trying to seduce this Cerberus who did not, I thought, have a mean enough look to go with the ferocious reputation with which he had been saddled. If it had been a Doberman Pinscher I might have had second thoughts. Also the beast was thin.

Collecting the bread I had saved for my breakfast and a small piece of chocolate from a Red Cross parcel, I went and sat close to where the dog was scratching himself in the sun and pretended to be eating the bread with every manifestation of relish and a good deal of noise. The dog was instantly alert and obviously deeply interested. I paid no attention to him and, after a short time devoted to intense thought, he got up and came closer. Then he sat down again and eyed me with interest. After a little while I started talking to him partly in English (which can sound more soothing than German) and partly in German in case he missed the finer points of what I had to say. My imitation of someone enjoying a rather horrible piece of German ration bread must have been pretty convincing for, after a short pause, he started dribbling, then he wagged his tail in a tentative way. When I offered him a bit of bread he came and took it very politely and sat down close to me. By the time we got to the chocolate we were buddies. His name was Fritz.

It now only remained to get rid of his handler. I found this ornament of the SS in the guardroom reading the *Völkischer Beobachter*, the official Party paper (which cannot have been very encouraging literature at this stage of the war) and asked him why he had not gone off with his mates while the going was good.

'It's Untersturmführer Bader,' he grumbled, 'he said I had to stay because of the dog. He says it has to be here to stop you people from escaping at night.'

'Rubbish,' I said, 'who wants to escape when all we have to do is to sit and wait until our friends come and fetch us? Of course,' I added 'they'll find you here too, won't they? I must say, I wouldn't like to be an SS man caught on duty in a concentration camp by the British or the Americans. They'll shoot you on the spot. But then, of course, it may be the French who get here first. They won't shoot you, they'll just tear you apart.'

'But Bader will shoot me if I go!'

'If you've already gone, idiot, how can he shoot you? If I were you I'd go now, while he's out looking for motor coaches. Have you got your civilian clothes ready and your false papers?'

'Yes, I have.'

'Well my advice is go and get them and shove off before Bader gets back, but,' I added, 'you can't take the dog.'

'But I can't stop him – he'll just follow me.'

'That's all right,' I said, 'I'll look after Fritz.'

'But he won't obey anyone but me.'

Right on cue Fritz strolled into the guardroom, gave his handler a rather cold look, and came and put his paws on my shoulders soliciting chocolate.

'Go on,' I said to the handler, 'Fritz and I will go into my hut and you get out while the going's good.'

Fritz and I sat in the door of my hut and, within fifteen minutes, the handler was plodding down the road to Innsbruck and was soon out of sight. Fritz watched him go with no sign of emotion at all.

From then on Fritz shared my bed for as long as we were in Reichenau. Unfortunately when we left he had gone off somewhere and I never saw him again. Bader never found out that Fritz was no longer on the job. I think he was too scared of him to go out and look.

With no electric fence and Fritz safe in my bed there was nothing to stop anybody from escaping if they felt so inclined. On reflection, however, it seemed a futile thing to do. The war could not possibly last more than a few days, there was no food to take for the journey, it was bitterly cold at night and I personally was much too weak from undernourishment to travel any distance.

There was also another consideration. If Bader were to discover that one of his charges was missing, he would be perfectly capable of killing the lot on the plea that we were about to fall into enemy hands. Nobody was likely to count the corpses.

This may sound far-fetched but it must be remembered that Bader was one of the dangerously stupid men of which there were so many in the Gestapo. It would not occur to him that if he were at fault there would be nobody to call him to account except Stiller, who could also be liquidated, and above Stiller – no-one at all. Also he was bestial and Nazi enough to feel great satisfaction in killing so many obvious enemies of his Führer.

He belonged to the same category as the fanatical SS who, when the war was already irrevocably lost and the Allies pressing on into Germany, still blew up bridges and destroyed buildings on the principle that if the Third Reich was not to enjoy them, then nobody would. They brought inconvenience, misery and often death to none but their own fellow Germans. They refused to surrender towns which were of no strategic or tactical value to anybody. In so doing they delayed a small part of the Allied armies for perhaps twenty-four hours and the towns, which would otherwise have been undamaged, were reduced to rubble during the softening-up bombardment before the assault. I have visited such towns where the remaining inhabitants with no other accommodation but the more solidly constructed cellars were understandably resentful. Having seen Coventry and Plymouth I had little sympathy for them, but one can see their point of view.

One of us who did actually take the trouble to escape from this camp was Jack Churchill. He was, of course, technically doing his duty as an officer and I also believe that even if escape were not possible until the very last moment, he would still have found it intolerable to be liberated by somebody else. In fact, he did not reach Naples until after Peter Churchill and I had left there for England. His departure also made it necessary for us to take measures to cover up the fact that we were one short, an exercise in which the Greek generals played a leading part on the one occasion on which Stiller and Bader decided to count their chickens.

Our party was now complete and only the lack of diesel-engined transport held up our departure for the Southern Redoubt. There were now 136 hostages (men, women and children) and fifty-one guards made up of Stiller, Bader and forty-nine other ranks.

One SS man was quite different from the others. He was a polite, well-spoken young man, an Austrian and by profession an opera singer. It appeared that he had never wanted to get into the SS, or the army either for that matter, but had been drafted into this organisation when he was called up, and he hated it. It was only towards the end of the war that the SS had been obliged to resort to conscription to maintain its strength, all members until then having been volunteers. This particular man was of great value to us for his sympathies were all on our side and, in this way, we had a reliable informer inside the enemy camp. When the end came for the SS we made sure that this young man was not included in their number.

There was a small group of us now among the hostages made up of people who, rather than let things drift and hope for the best, were watching events very carefully and making plans to deal with whatever turn they might take. This group had a distinctly international flavour and included 'Wings' Day, Peter Churchill, Müller, Falkenhausen, Schlabrendorf, Liedig, Garibaldi and Ferrero, myself and one or two others. Taken all round we added up to a good deal more brainpower than Stiller and Bader could muster between them which, as things turned out, was just as well. It was by laying our heads together and summarising all the information which in our various ways we had been able to acquire that we were able to build up a clear picture of the situation and the future intentions of the Gestapo, and plan accordingly.

Briefly the position was this: 136 hostages had been gathered together and 135 of them were being taken into the Southern Redoubt under the escort of a party of SS led by two officers, one of whom (the dominant character of the two) was a killer.

Simultaneously the Redoubt was to be garrisoned by Waffen-SS divisions (combat units of the SS). Finally, certain Nazi leaders would enter the sanctuary and bargain for their lives and liberty against that of the hostages. From the Nazi point of view defence would not involve more than preventing the infiltration of raiding parties and of taking the fortress by surprise.

Any more frontal attack by the Allies, involving artillery or aerial bombardment, would endanger the lives of the hostages who, according to the completely fallacious reasoning of the Germans, were of overriding importance to the Allies.

Should the Nazi leaders or the garrison fail to reach the Southern Redoubt, the hostages were to be liquidated under arrangements made by Bader.

So far the position was clear. It remained to assess what was likely to happen and make arrangements accordingly. In this we were greatly assisted by the fact that I had relieved one of the absconding guards of his portable radio with which we were able to keep abreast of events as reported in the German war bulletins.

Things were moving fast. Berlin fell to the Russians on the 25th April, Eisenhower had a bridgehead across the Elbe at Magdeburg, Montgomery had taken Hamburg and was cleaning up north-west Germany, Field Marshal Model had surrendered the Ruhr and, fifty miles south of Berlin, Russian and American advance guards had met at Torgau. In the south the Russians were at Klagenfurt at the eastern end of the Puster Tal and the French were hurrying along the Swiss border to the northern end of the Brenner. In Italy the final collapse had begun.

There were confusing and often contradictory statements by the German High Command, apparently authoritative announcements being made sometimes by Goering, sometimes by Admiral Raeder, sometimes by others. The one thing that seemed certain was that Hitler was no longer in the saddle and the voice of Goebbels was heard no more. Actually, although we did not know it, it was at about this time that Hitler shot first Eva Braun and then himself, and Goebbels fulfilled the promise he had made on New Year's Day and poisoned his wife, his children and himself.

It seemed most unlikely that the Nazi leaders who were to use the Southern Redoubt would ever get there and still more improbable that the SS divisions would turn up to defend it. Falkenhausen and Halder declared categorically that, if there were any Wehrmacht units in the Puster Tal, they would most certainly refuse to have anything to do with the hostages scheme. They would in fact be far more likely actively to oppose it. It seemed, therefore, that of the three parties heading for the Southern Redoubt ours would be the only one to make it. I learned after the war that Goering did in fact fly in but, finding it un-garrisoned, left again to try and lose himself in Germany.

Our planning was thus limited to dealing with one contingency only: to prevent the Gestapo from carrying out their extermination orders and to subsist until the Allies reached us to take us home, make sure they knew where we were and arrived as soon as possible.

After careful consideration of all aspects of the situation, we decided to let the Gestapo take us into the Puster Tal, where Garibaldi was certain that he would be able to make contact with the local resistance movement. This would give us some outside contact at least and possibly a direct link with the advancing Allies.

I calculate that we left Innsbruck on the 28th April 1945. Stiller had at last been able to raise three diesel coaches with enough fuel to take us the 120 kilometres which lay before us and, with his army truck, we were able to travel in comfort. A few SS travelled in each coach and the remainder piled into the lorry.

The trip to the summit was long and tedious for there was a great deal of traffic coming the other way and in those days there was no Autobahn in Austria. We made it at last. We all got out and stood around while the engines cooled off for they were not in good condition and the quality of the fuel probably left much to be desired. It was a little disturbing during this pause to hear the almost incessant bursting of bombs and rattle of machine-gun and cannon fire from the southern side of the pass. Germans moving north told us that traffic was under constant attack from bombers and low-flying fighters.

We even considered staying where we were, but dealing with Bader would have been difficult there, and we would have suffered greatly from the cold at 4,500 feet. Also, we had no food.

I must confess that personally my main fear was that, having survived over two years in the hands of the Gestapo with my life (at least in the earlier stages) not worth a red cent, I might be killed at the very end by a British or American bomb or bullet.

We moved on at about midday when there was a lull in the traffic and it seemed that at this stage in the war the Allied air forces knocked off for lunch, for we never saw a single aircraft all the way down the pass. For this we were truly thankful.

As soon as we entered the Puster Tal we could see that it had indeed been prepared to withstand a siege. There were tank traps across the valley, pillboxes had been built at strategic points and the mouth of each side valley was similarly defended. Our forecast was however correct. There was no sign of any garrison, SS or otherwise, manning these defences.

There was a certain amount of traffic along the valley in both directions but it all seemed aimless and disorganised. Germans in Italy who could raise a car and the necessary petrol were trying desperately to get back to Germany with the intention of submerging into the civilian population and so avoiding an indeterminate sojourn as prisoners of war. Many doubtless hoped to find and succour their families, already living under conditions they knew to be bad and which were sure to become worse.

There were a lot of superior looking staff cars, usually filled with five or six very young officers. These fugitives from the battle area were certainly following the valley to avoid the hazards of air attack in the Brenner but, in early Spring, there is no easy way out of the Puster Tal west of Klagenfurt and that was already in the hands of the Russians. So, thwarted in that direction, they were turning back for the Brenner, no doubt preferring the hazards of air attack to the prospect of Siberia as prisoners of war of the Russians.

In the middle of the afternoon we drew up by the side of the road, a few hundred yards from the village of Niederdorf, which stood astride the main road. On the maps of today (this part of the Tyrol having been handed back to Italy) the names are only shown in Italian and Niederdorf has become Villabassa, but even in 1945 the local inhabitants appeared to use only the Italian form.

Having enjoined us not to leave the coaches, Stiller and Bader set off for the village and, after a decent interval, the bolder amongst us followed. Protests from the guards were ignored, a risk we would certainly not have taken had Bader been there. The first building we came to was the inn on the edge of the village square into which we trooped demanding coffee and beer. Surprisingly this was served just as if we had been peacetime tourists. Although the coffee was ersatz, it was quite good – which only went to show that the concentration camp cooks could have done a great deal better if they had taken the trouble!

There were quite a few people in the coffee room, military and civilian, which was just as well because Stiller and Bader were sitting at a table in a corner. When they saw us come in Stiller looked upset and Bader furious but in front of so many witnesses there was nothing they could do about it. Having enjoyed our drinks and told the waitress that the SS gentlemen in the corner over there would pay the bill, we strolled back to the coaches.

Stiller came back a little later to say that he had arranged for us to stay the night in the village. The women, children and old men would sleep at the inn and the remainder would go to the Rathaus, or town hall. There were no beds, he said apologetically, but he had seen to it that there was plenty of clean straw.

When we were finally installed, it was clear that all the men who might be expected to make trouble were gathered together in the Rathaus and had been given an extraordinarily generous amount of straw to sleep on. We were not grateful but discussed how well the straw would burn and how effective such a fire would be if it happened to occur in the middle of the night when we were safely locked in. We were on the first floor of the building and it was a long drop to the ground. We decided to post a watch to give the alarm if necessary and to take remedial action in the morning.

Chapter 15

The Southern Redoubt

A castle called Doubting Castle, the
owner whereof was Giant Despair.
John Bunyan

T he first thing to happen the following morning was that Stiller
and Bader decided to count their flock. Fortunately, after the
departure of Jack Churchill, this hazard had been foreseen and
prepared for. I have already related how, in the basement of the hotel in
Naples, we had amused ourselves by confusing the officer trying to count
us. On that occasion the principal performer had been a French girl playing the changes with her headscarf and the object had been simply to
annoy.

This time the matter was a great deal more serious. Instead of just getting varying numbers it was essential that the Gestapo would arrive at
first go at the exact number they were expecting – 136. If they got the
true figure of 135 we would be in trouble. If they got too many we would
be no better off for Bader was quite sharp enough to put us all in a bunch
surrounded by guards and get the true score by counting us out like sheep
through a gate. Our plan depended on him not choosing this method first.

They did their counting the way we hoped they would. They assem-
bled all the hostages in the village square, lined us up in two rows and
counted heads.

By fortunate coincidence four of the Greek generals rather looked
like each other each other in height and build and their uniforms
strongly resembled those of the British so, plus Colonels McGrath and
Churchill, the Gestapo would be expecting seven people in Allied army
uniform and our deceiving tactics were based on a precision of movement worthy of the ballet.

Three generals stood together at the beginning of the front rank, Papagos was about halfway down it and the fifth general and McGrath were near the beginning of the rear rank. Without letting any of them into the secret we had been able to manoeuvre so that the women and children were down at the end of both ranks and some of the largest men made up the first part of the front rank. The stage was set.

Stiller and Bader walked slowly down the front line counting carefully. When they were about halfway along, the third Greek general slipped unostentatiously backwards, through the rear rank between his colleague and McGrath and bobbed up again in the middle of the back row.

Having counted the front line from left to right Stiller and Bader now started on the rear from right to left and got three officers in khaki. They had already had four in the front rank, $4 + 3 = 7$, and everybody was happy. As they walked away number one Greek moved back to the front rank to restore the original picture and the exercise was over.

With sighs of relief we realised that the deception had been successful – and then came the bombshell. After comparing notes with Stiller, Bader announced we were one short. After the shock, however, came the anti-climax. One of the Sippenhäftlinge announced innocently that her mother was not feeling well and had stayed in bed. Stiller and Bader seemed as relieved as we were, if for different reasons.

Stiller then announced that for the rest of the day we would be free to move around on the village square, but warned us that he was posting sentries at every exit and that anybody attempting to leave it would be shot on sight, without the formality of a prior challenge.

The next items on the agenda were to attend to our safety and to let the Allies know of our existence and where to find us.

For the first of these we had decided that our best hope was to try and enlist the help of a Wehrmacht unit if we could find one in the valley, cashing in on the hatred and contempt of the army for the SS. Falkenhausen would be charged with this mission.

For both problems – communication with the Allies and information on local German units – the answer seemed to be the local partisans, if we could get in touch with them. This was Garibaldi's job but without being able to leave the village square it was difficult to see how he could make contact.

Pondering the problem Garibaldi, Ferrero and I were pacing up and down and the square and I was getting more and more irritated by Garibaldi's rhetorical pleas for guidance, addressed more or less indiscriminately to God, the Devil, Ferrero and me.

'But how the Hell can I contact them?' he kept muttering. 'I'm absolutely certain they are in the valley but how to get in touch?'

'Oh, for God's sake,' I said at last rather unhelpfully, 'why don't you send them a postcard, or ring them up?'

Garibaldi stopped dead in his tracks.

'Why, of course!' he exclaimed. 'It's so simple I never thought of it!'

Kissing me rapidly on both cheeks, he set off at a fast trot for the village post office with Ferrero and me in hot pursuit.

The post office, naturally enough, was in the middle of one side of the square, about halfway between two sets of our guards so there was nothing to stop us from going in. Garibaldi shot inside and asked the old lady behind the counter for the telephone exchange. She pointed to a door behind her and, with a quick word of assurance to the startled dame from Ferrero, behind the counter we all went and into the room at the back. Here there was an antique switchboard and another old lady sitting in front of it with a headset perched on her grey hair. There was also a young Wehrmacht sentry who was brusquely ordered to get out as we had private business to transact. He left without a murmur.

'Put me through to the partisan headquarters,' said Garibaldi, tapping the old dear on the shoulder.

'Certainly, Signore,' she replied, as unruffled as if he had asked for the local butcher. She pushed in a plug, twiddled the handle, then shoved in another plug.

'The partisans,' she announced calmly, handing the headset to Garibaldi.

There followed an explosion of Italian which lasted for several minutes. Finally Garibaldi handed the apparatus back to the old lady, patted her on the head, and back we went to the sunshine of the square.

'Very satisfactory,' said Garibaldi. 'The leader of the local partisans and his adjutant will meet us here in the square in about half an hour. Also, he says there is a German area commander with some infantry units at Dobbiaco, so Falkenhausen can get cracking.'

Within the hour two dangerous looking ruffians turned up in homburg hats. That they were partisans was manifest from the surprising fact that each carried a Sten gun over his shoulder. It was a telling illustration of the degree of apathy and confusion in the German ranks at this stage of the war that two civilians, carrying offensive weapons as obviously British as Sten guns, could walk about openly and unchallenged in broad daylight.

It was at once arranged that 'Wings' Day should leave with our new friends who would lead him through to the Allied lines so that he could report our presence and whereabouts. At the same time he would try to arrange a direct link up between the partisans' wireless and Allied Headquarters. He left the same day.

It now remained to take steps to avoid being exterminated, which could only be achieved by neutralising our SS escort and, particularly, Bader.

Since the partisans had confirmed that there was a German area commander at Dobbiaco, our original plan to enlist the Wehrmacht on our side was confirmed and Falkenhausen was detailed to put it into execution. Posting himself by the side of the road where it ran through the square, he waited for a suitable vehicle to turn up. After ignoring a couple of old bangers which he clearly thought to be beneath his dignity, he stopped a fine staff car travelling east with five young officers in it.

There was no problem. When a general in full canonicals signals to a car-load of young subalterns to stop – it stops. With the exception of the driver the young hopefuls were ordered out of the vehicle, Falkenhausen installed himself in the back, and off he sailed out of the square on the road to Dobbiaco. The SS guards never even noticed the departure of one of their wards in a style they certainly did not expect.

We then settled down to await results and, shortly after lunch, we got them.

Wehrmacht soldiers armed with automatic weapons suddenly appeared at each entrance to the square, the SS sentries were disarmed, and the whole lot herded into the area in front of the town hall. Then a very tall captain, accompanied by Falkenhausen, drove up in a very small car and lined up the whole Gestapo gang under the supervision of his men. When the SS had been disarmed completely, he stepped across to us, clicked his heels, saluted and introduced himself.

'Alvensleben, commanding the 9th Assault Company of Infantry.'

'Good afternoon, captain,' I replied. 'Are you by any chance a relation of the Herr von Alvensleben who was President of the Herrenklub?'

'My uncle, Herr Major. Have you any news of him? I heard that he had been arrested.'

'Yes,' I told him, 'he was in the cells at Buchenwald.'

'Do you know what happened to him?'

I knew very well what had happened to him. Shortly before we left Buchenwald he had been removed to the civil prison in Weimar and was by now almost certainly a free man. However, it seemed a pity to miss an opportunity of adding fuel to his nephew's dislike of the Gestapo. I looked embarrassed.

'Well,' I said, 'you know what the Gestapo are like. He was a charming old man, and I'm very sorry.'

Actually the old man had been a continuously grumbling and complaining old bore and we were glad to see the back of him.

'Yes,' said Alvensleben between his teeth, 'I know what they are like.'

After a short pause for hate he went on: 'I am about to send this lot off towards the Brenner in their truck – unarmed of course – and after that they can look after themselves. Before they go have you any particular complaints?'

The Greek generals had been constantly protesting that they had lost their luggage and this seemed as good a complaint as any. Personally I had no luggage to lose.

'Yes, they have stolen our luggage.'

Alvensleben turned to his sergeant and pointed to the SS truck.

'Search it,' he snapped.

There was no Greek generals' luggage but, what was a great deal more welcome, there were about two hundred Red Cross parcels.

Alvensleben looked almost happy. 'Unload it,' he ordered.

The sergeant picked a working party who, with obvious relish, quickly emptied the truck completely. Red Cross parcels, suitcases and fuel cans were piled up on the ground, and last to come out were a couple of rather blowsy looking women. The SS believed in taking their amenities on tour with them.

It only remained to say that we wanted to keep the opera singer and that the rest could go. They were herded into their truck, the direction was pointed out to them and, under the threat of the Wehrmacht rifles, they departed and we saw them no more.

As soon as Garibaldi heard what was to be done with our late escort he made a rush for the post office to ring up his partisan pals and tell them what was happening. And particularly that a truck carrying fifty unarmed SS would shortly be travelling down the valley from Villabassa towards the Brenner.

It was later reported that a number of corpses were to be seen dangling from the trees by the side of the road, but whether this was in fact true I cannot tell.

I do know that on the following day, wearing his Sten gun like a status symbol, a rather down at heel partisan visited us with a number of watches he was trying to flog.

It took some time to realise that now, for the first time since January 1943, I was nobody's prisoner. There was no longer any threat to my life or liberty, and I was free to do what I liked. I think the bell rang when we had a conference with the partisan leader as to what we should do until our friends came to fetch us, and I was presented with a fine Lüger pistol. It was Monday, 30th April 1945.

Our main problem was where to live until the arrival of the rescue party. The partisan leader and Alvensleben both advised retiring to some safe place which the Wehrmacht company could easily defend against any possible Gestapo reprisals, for Bader was not a man to give up easily. While one liked to think that he was adorning a tree on the Brunico road, this was by no means certain.

It appeared that Falkenhausen had painted the local commander so glowing a picture of our importance to the Allies and forecast so dreadful a fate for the senior German officer in the area if a hair of our heads was harmed, that Alvensleben had received specific instructions in writing (very legibly signed by the commander, no doubt with an eye to the acquisition of merit) that his last and greatest mission in this war was to defend us all against the Gestapo or any other aggressor to the last round and the last man. It only remained for us to facilitate this admirable task.

The partisan chief advised us to move to a nearby hotel, isolated in the forest beside a little lake and easy to defend. The place was called 'Lago di Braies' – or less euphonically in German 'Pragser Wildsee'. A quick reconnaissance in Alvensleben's car showed the place to be a luxury hotel, fully furnished and, while there was no central heating or hot water because the boilers had burst, there would be no difficulty in keeping warm for there were stoves and plenty of wood to burn in them.

The move was made the same evening using the coaches which the Gestapo had not been allowed to take with them. There were no drivers, of course, but there were plenty among us who could cope and, while some were clearly not used to manoeuvring motor coaches, we managed very well. I drove the front coach but I have forgotten who drove the other two. It was about ten kilometres from the village to the hotel, the last eight of them up a narrow lane in very bad repair and twisting and climbing steeply through the pine woods, but we made it in fine style and mostly in bottom gear.

As soon as we had arrived and chosen our rooms, Alvensleben reported for orders, so we went round together and posted sentries so as to deny all unauthorised entry into the hotel area.

I remember thinking at the time how remarkably things had changed in a few hours. We – at least those of us who were not Germans – were now protected by the army of a country with which we were still at war from attack by another armed service of that same country. The sentries being posted were charged, not with keeping us in, but with keeping the Gestapo out. Their orders were that we were to be permitted to pass at will and they were to present arms to any 'prisoners' who approached. This last was at my suggestion, partly from vanity and partly to ensure that the sentries really understood who they were protecting and who they were to shoot – but this did have one rather unfortunate result.

On the following day little Maria-Dolores von Schuschnigg, who had never been free in her life and had learned to shun anybody in a field-grey uniform, went toddling off to look at the lake. At a turn in the path she came unexpectedly upon a sentry who, in strict compliance with his orders, produced a crashing salute which sent the terrified child screaming to her mother.

That evening our communications section – the partisans' clandestine wireless unit – moved in and our headquarters was complete. The set was installed on the top floor where reception would be best and one of Alvensleben's men was detailed as runner to bring us any messages which might come in.

It only remained to organise the commissariat for now we were on our own. We had no shortage of cooks for every German lady, however blue-blooded, is a *Hausfrau* at heart and for once there was no short-age of food either. With 200 Red Cross parcels for 134 people plus the Sippenhäftling stocks we calculated that it would not be necessary to introduce rationing for the short time we would have to look after our-selves. That night there were a good many upset stomachs from eating too much – and not only eating. Before the day was out the partisans had turned up with a large quantity of red wine and several bottles of grappa – luxuries (if grappa can be so defined) to which we had long been unaccustomed.

The following day certain minor problems had to be dealt with. One of these was that the wireless section wanted a spare battery and the simplest way of getting one seemed to be to commandeer a car. I got Alvensleben's driver to take me down to the main road and from there, my Lüger handy in my pocket, I walked a few hundred yards toward Brunico and sat down on a convenient boulder.

The first few cars which came along looked and sounded terrible and their batteries were definitely on their last legs, so I let them go. Then came a convoy of three cars together which I was not prepared to tackle singlehanded. After about half an hour, however, quite a good looking Mercedes showed up so, putting on the German helmet I had borrowed from the driver, I stepped into the road and waved it down. To my great relief it stopped.

Producing my pistol, I then invited the occupants to get out, which they did. They were all Feldgendarmerie with the brass plates which for some reason or other the German military police wore hanging round their necks on a chain, like decanters (one expected them to be engraved 'port' or 'sherry'). I lined them up along the side of the road, told them to lay down their arms and get walking towards Brunico. At first their leader seemed inclined to argue but a bullet between his feet made him change his mind. Actually he did not know how lucky he was, for I am not a good shot with a pistol. They turned and trudged wearily away down the road with all the apathy of a defeated army.

The car was in very good condition so, stopping only to give the driver his helmet back and tell him to return to Lago di Braies, I drove my prize back to headquarters. Its battery was then handed over to the wireless operators, theirs was put in the Mercedes for recharging and the driver was made responsible for ensuring that the partisans always had a charged battery at their disposal. It was really a very good car and when we left the hotel I gave it to Garibaldi, who was duly grateful.

During the day the wireless section announced that they were in contact with the Allies who appeared to know all about us, so it seemed certain that 'Wings' Day had already accomplished his mission.

I spent the rest of the afternoon sitting in the sun by the lake arguing theology with Martin Niemoeller. My father had been a Presbyterian minister and, from an early age, I had been accustomed to hear him discuss comparative religion with his friends of all denominations. I had also learned to debate both religion and politics without allowing it to degenerate into dispute.

Martin was a very curious man. A U-boat commander in the First World War, he was a firm believer in the principle of 'my country right or wrong' and, even after having been slung into a concentration camp by the Nazis, he still volunteered to return to the submarine service when the Second World War broke out. His offer was refused. This, however, was not the subject of our discussion.

Niemoeller started it by stating that world movements of population always took place from east to west, against the direction of rotation of the Earth, illustrating his point by reference to the Huns, Genghis Khan and the emigrations from Europe to the Americas. So far, I was not prepared to argue.

Then, however, he sought to explain this unilateral tendency with the analogy of a fly walking on an orange. If the orange is gently rotated, the fly (or so he declared) will always walk against the direction of rotation. Never having experimented with fly-infested oranges I was still not prepared to argue although I did remark that, in my experience, as soon as you put your hand anywhere near an object supporting a fly, the fly took off on the turn.

A man on the surface of the Earth is subject to the gravity of the Earth while the fly on the orange is also subject to it as well as, infinitesimally, to the pull exerted by the mass of the orange. I did, however, point out that his analogy did not theoretically hold water. Martin then shot off at a tangent with a statement which, coming from a militant evangelical parson, surprised me a lot.

The lives of all of us on Earth, he declared, are influenced by the movements of the stars, simply because the mass of the stars must exert a pull on the human brain. I argued that, enormous though many of the stars are compared with the Earth, the effect of their weight when divided by the square of a few hundred light years must be pretty negligible. This he would not concede – an attitude which, in a man who must have mastered at least enough mathematics to navigate his submarine, I could only ascribe to pig-headedness.

The discussion, lubricated by a bottle of grappa and with Peter Churchill occasionally intervening, lasted until supper time when, the grappa having proved more potent than Martin had supposed, Peter and I had to put him to bed. Niemoeller and I met again on several later occasions but we have discussed neither theology, astrology nor mass movements of population.

That evening I found an old radio set in the hotel which was not restricted to receiving only Deutschlandsender and for the first time since the beginning of 1943 I was able to listen to the BBC. This was the first time I heard that enchanting tune 'Lillibulero'. In the various countries in which we have lived since we have always listened to the BBC news on the World Service and this tune never fails to remind me of Lago di Braies, and particularly of the evening of the 3rd May 1945.

That evening I invited Alvensleben and his two senior sergeants to come and listen to the BBC. Sure enough, the capitulation of all the German forces in Italy which had occurred the previous day on 2 May was announced and, for us, the war was over.

It is difficult to imagine a more emotional occasion. The German NCOs wept unashamedly and, for us, it was hard to realise that the moment we had waited for so long – for some freedom after five years of captivity or more – had actually come. There seems to be a limit to the amount of shock or emotion the human mind can absorb at one time – which is probably just as well. I had experienced this when I was captured in 1943, and now there was the counter-shock that all my troubles were over.

Later that evening we received a message through the partisan wireless that the Americans would be with us at eight o'clock on the following morning.

At a quarter to eight next day, in accordance with my instructions, Captain von Alvensleben paraded his men on the drive outside the hotel entrance and, marching in single file through one door into the foyer, they deposited helmets, gas masks, arms, side arms and ammunition in neat piles and marched out through the other door. Then they formed up again outside to await the moment of surrender.

At eight o'clock precisely the first American Jeeps appeared among the trees, advancing with the greatest care. What they expected to find

I had no idea, but they were clearly prepared to overcome resistance for their advance was a model of well covered movement. Then I remembered that 'Wings' Day had left before our Gestapo had been disposed of by the Wehrmacht and they could not know that we were now being defended rather than confined. I was almost sorry that we had disarmed the Germans before the United States Army arrived when, after their precautions, the Americans broke cover in front of the hotel to find the enemy meekly paraded and without arms. On the other hand, it was probably better that way. Some trigger-happy GI might have lost his head and somebody might have been hurt.

The first thing the American officer in command did was to ask the non-German members of the party if we would mind staying on a couple of extra days. This was to give the intelligence officers time to catalogue the Germans among the hostages which would have been very difficult without our help. It was strongly suspected that there were some among them who were wanted as war criminals and, to my knowledge, General von Falkenhausen, Fritz Thyssen and Hjalmar Schacht subsequently stood trial. We naturally agreed.

During the morning a big convoy of very large trucks came thundering up the hill through the trees and drew up on the lawn beside the lake. This, we were told, was the bath unit. At that time, of course, none of us had any experience of the luxury which accompanies the United States Army when it goes to war, and this outfit was a revelation. In a very short time three marquees had sprung up, a pump was drawing water from the lake, there was hot water in the showers, and we were invited to make use of the facilities – women and children first.

When my turn came I was amazed. It seems that in the US Army the soldier has very little clothing which is actually his own property. When he enters the bath unit he just hands in his dirty shirt, socks, pants, battledress and what have you in the first tent, emerges clean and naked from the showers in the second tent where he had been issued with soap and a towel and, clutching his few personal possessions, draws a complete new outfit in the third tent. All he has to do is to remember what sizes he takes.

For us the procedure was the same except that some of us had items of clothing we were determined not to lose. Prince Xavier had sworn to return to France wearing his blue and grey prison stripes and I had no intention of being separated from my patched shirt, my battledress blouse or my flannel trousers. This did not, of course, prevent us from acquiring a clean outfit as well.

Our last days at Lago di Braies were odd and restless. We were finally liberated, the war was over, but we were not yet on the way home. Part of the time was spent helping the intelligence officers who were investigating the German contingent and part in talking to the Press correspondents, who had turned up in force. The Americans had put up a volleyball net and we played a little but we were still in no condition to be particularly energetic. We wandered about rather aimlessly most of the time, smoking far too many American cigarettes and waiting for something to happen.[1]

It was during this time that our strength went down by four. The first to disappear were the young Belgian pilot and Heidi. Why they went off they did not reveal nor do I know how they fared. It is quite possible that they wanted to avoid the separation which would have been inevitable, probably for quite a long time, had they stayed with us.

The next to go were Kokorin and Bessonov. Kokorin had been very upset by the death of his friend Dietrich Bonhöffer and now he was terrified of returning to Russia, a dread he shared with Bessonov. It seemed that returning prisoners of war were not welcome in the Soviet Union and that awkward questions were asked about how they had got themselves captured. I heard after the war that Bessonov, who did go back to Russia, was tried and shot. Kokorin never attempted to go back. He went over to the Balkans and joined some resistance movement. He died a year or two later from frostbite and exposure.

I tried to pass the dragging hours by collecting the signatures of some of the more interesting characters present, which I thought might be an intriguing souvenir of this phase of my captivity – such people as Léon Blum, Kallay (the Prime Minister of Hungary), Horthy (son of the famous Hungarian admiral), Schuschnigg and so on.

When I came to Schacht he offered to enrich my paper in exchange for a bar of Red Cross chocolate and was considerably offended when I said it was not worth it. I was amused to read some years later, in Sefton Delmer's book *The Germans and I* that Schacht repeated exactly the same gambit with the press correspondents who wanted to interview him after his acquittal at Nuremberg, only this time it was interviews in exchange for chocolate.

The day ended at last, as even the longest days must, and we were asked to be ready to leave at nine o'clock next morning.

Chapter 16

The Road to Freedom

Freedom has a thousand charms to show,
That slaves, howe'er contented, never know.
William Cowper

The 8th May 1945 started with the arrival at Lago di Braies of a fleet of US Army command cars. These vehicles, rather like very oversized Jeeps, were surprisingly comfortable. As far as I can remember each one took four of us so it must have been an impressive convoy which set out for the south.

Garibaldi and Ferrero left independently in the Mercedes I had given them, accompanied by a quite remarkably beautiful young Italian soldier called Amici. When the Sachsenhausen Sonderlager was created it was designed on the principles of a prisoner of war camp for officers, so a few soldiers were posted to it as batmen. This was why the Irishmen Walsh and Cushing were there (and now with us) and also young Amici.

I do not know under what circumstances he had been incarcerated. It may be that he was arrested after the first Italian capitulation. The most interesting fact about him was that his elder brother was the American film star Don Ameche, which no doubt accounted for our Amici's good looks. He explained that when his brother had gone to Hollywood he had altered the spelling of the family name in the vain hope that in its revised form it would be correctly pronounced by the Americans.

Before the convoy set off there was a great deal of acrimonious argument among the Sippenhäftlinge about seating arrangements. It appeared that in a chauffeur-driven car there was a certain loss of face involved in sitting beside the driver. On the part of people who were, after all, on the losing side this was petty and intolerable. They were smartly cut down to size and bundled in as they came.

The Sippenhäftlinge having been promptly subdued by a brusque invitation to get on board or be left behind, we set off down the Puster Tal in considerably better spirits than when we came up it a few days earlier. For one thing we were really free. For another for the first time in years we had eaten as much as we could – and probably more than we should. For us the war was over and we were going home.

We set off shortly after nine o'clock, comfortably installed in the command cars which, being open, gave us the full benefit of the Dolomite scenery. It was a fine sunny day. I think the Spring of 1945 must have been unusually clement altogether for I remember no bad weather at all from the time we left Buchenwald. Yet my wife recalls that in Cheltenham, on the first of May, it was snowing.

After we had passed Bressanone progress was not at all rapid for the road was seriously encumbered with vehicles destroyed by air attack and by Allied troops moving north into Germany. We were not, however, in any particular hurry. We were due to spend the night in Verona and to fly on to Naples the next day, and from Villabassa to Verona is only about 250 kilometres (155 miles).

It is significant that I have no recollection of lunch that day. Until the arrival of the Americans the lack of food had played so important a part in our lives that every detail was memorable. Now, full fed three times a day with snacks in between, meals were no longer of particular significance and so were quickly forgotten. Such is the ingratitude of man. I expect we had a substantial picnic by the side of the road.

It was late afternoon when we arrived in Verona and went straight to a hotel which looked like the set for a Renaissance film. For some reason it is connected in my mind with *Romeo and Juliet*.

Perhaps I was told that the 1936 film of the play by George Cukor had sets built from specially researched photographs of Verona? There was no shortage of suitable balconies!

That evening we had a proper meal in the hotel restaurant. There were white tablecloths and napkins, proper glass and cutlery, real waiters, and it was wonderful. Peter Churchill and I shared a room with a private bath and even the water was hot. There was no doubt about it – we were back in the fleshpots.

Next morning after a reasonable breakfast we drove to the airfield where several Dakotas were waiting for us. The organisation was perfect, there were no delays. Within minutes we were airborne and heading south.

The military Dakota was not an ideally comfortable passenger aeroplane, having been designed to carry troops rather than tycoons, but it was a very great improvement on the last flight I had made, sitting on the floor of a Ju52 from Tunis to Naples, chained to the airframe.

The captain of our aircraft was a most amiable young man who must, I think, have been told something of our circumstances, for he could not have been more anxious to make our journey interesting. Either he or his co-pilot frequently came back to point out to us places of interest on the ground, and he usually made a detour to help us to see better. Flying in those days was, of course, a far more carefree method of travel than it is today, and pilots were a great deal less tied to flight plans, routes, altitudes and the radio.

We had a good look at Florence, circled over Rome, and then made a slight diversion to the east of our direct route to Naples to Monte Cassino.

This was the place we were all most eager to see for, of all the places mentioned in the course of the Italian campaign, this was the name which had figured most prominently. The pilot was most co-operative. He flew down to about a hundred feet above the ruins, then circled slowly, first one way and then the other, so that we could all have a really good view. It was a terrible sight.

This was the first time I had seen the result of a sustained combination of air bombardment and artillery fire. It seemed that what one spared, the other destroyed. Later, I was to see the same thing at Emmerich in Germany, which had been 'prepared' by bombers and artillery for the Canadian crossing of the Rhine.

I was looking at the time for accommodation for about thirty German Passport Control officials and I found absolutely nothing at all. In a town of about 50,000 inhabitants there was not a single building undamaged and 85 per cent were completely destroyed. What inhabitants were left had cleared holes for themselves in the cellars. I had to build new houses.

It was approaching midday when we landed at Capodichino airport near Naples and our arrival must have caused a certain amount of speculation among the ground staff – in fact, I know it did.

In 1970, to celebrate the 25th anniversary of the liberation of the hostages, the *Daily Telegraph* published an article of mine on the subject and a few days later a Mr Hattrell of Horley wrote to me as follows:

> I was at Air Traffic Control on Capodichino airport, Naples, and met, on American instructions, the party of people to whom your article refers. I have subsequently often wondered why people from such widely dispersed camps managed to be released by the Americans at one and the same time. I remember the party included relations near and distant of Count von Stauffenberg and General von Blohm.

If Mr Hattrell had been given the passenger list the name 'Stauffenberg' would certainly have stuck in his mind, for there were in fact nine of them, of all ages and both sexes. I can find no trace of the name 'Blohm' in the list of hostages, nor had I ever heard it. Could he have misread 'Léon Blum'?

Ochsensepp Müller recalls in his book *Bis zur letzten Konsequenz* that here again Doktor Hjalmar Schacht ran true to form. Some American officers, hearing that the famous ex-Finance Minister was among us, tried to get him to sign his name on dollar notes but this he would only do in exchange for cigarettes.

As soon as we disembarked the sheep were separated from the goats. All the Germans were taken away to be interned, pending investigation, on the Isle of Capri. We were whisked off to the British Repatriation Centre between Naples and Pompeii. So Heidi and her paramour had not been wrong to abscond from Lago di Braies if the uninterrupted continuation of their idyll was their dearest wish.

After a very British army lunch Peter and I proceeded to Naples to deal with our last outstanding problem. We were clean, full fed, as well dressed as we wished to be, but our hair left much to be desired. Mine had in fact been growing fast in all directions since it had last been cut by Karl in February, before we left Sachsenhausen, and Peter's was little better.

There was a shuttle service between the Centre and Naples which deposited us in front of the Officers' Club and there we found a hairdresser. By the time we had had our hair cut, shampooed, rubbed and massaged it was teatime so, until it was time to catch the shuttle back to the Centre, we sat on the terrace of a café, drank real coffee and watched the world go by. We were not short of money for when I gave the Mercedes to Garibaldi he had presented me with a large wad of lire he had got from the partisans. Where they got them from I did not want to know.

When we were back in the Centre we found a message for us to say that a car would be calling for us next morning to take us to Allied Headquarters at Caserta where the Intelligence people were anxious to talk to us. This was welcome news for we had heard disheartening talk in the Centre about how long it took to get a passage to England. It seemed that only sea transport was available and that there was a long waiting list so we hoped that in Headquarters we would find someone from SOE who could pull a crafty string on our behalf.

The adjutant of the Repatriation Centre was not at all helpful. For one thing he was probably continually pestered with sob stories from those who were tired of waiting, and for another he was annoyed with us for going off into Naples the day before without telling him first.

He did, however, promise to send off our telegrams to our people telling them that we were safe. Whether he did or not I do not know, but they never arrived.

The staff car duly turned up next morning and trundled us off to Caserta where we spent the day. A very busy morning answering questions for Intelligence was followed by lunch and another session with a wide variety of people.

In the ante-room before lunch we were introduced to an Air Marshal. This officer was returning to London next day in his personal Dakota and, as soon as he heard our history and learned of our present predicament, he promised to take us with him and to send a car to the Centre next morning to pick us up.

We then returned to the Centre where the adjutant received our statement that we would be leaving next day with a good deal of coolness and scepticism. He made it plain that if it came off (which he obviously doubted) we would have played a very dirty trick in jumping the queue in such a fashion. The poor chap was probably waiting to be repatriated himself.

Assuming a long delay awaiting a passage home we had intended to write letters that evening, confirming our telegrams and giving more detail of our escape, for we were in no doubt that we must both long ago have been written off as dead. Now there was no point. By flying back next day we would be in England long before any letters.

I was particularly anxious about my wife and daughter whom I had last seen in France in 1940 just before I set off for Dunkirk and they with my French in-laws fled south from the Somme to the Loire valley.

At first we had been able to keep in touch after I discovered that, although all postal services between England and France had been suspended, the Cable and Wireless Company was still accepting telegrams for the unoccupied zone of France and, what is more, getting them through.

I therefore cabled from time to time to a cousin of my wife who lived in Cahors. She in turn could send inter-zonal postcards to my wife and receive answers. A couple of French girls could send each other messages which meant a great deal more to them than to a German censor. Her cousin then sent me occasional postcards, most of which managed to find their way to me via Portugal. However, after the invasion of French North-west Africa in November 1942 the Germans occupied the whole of France, and all communication ceased.

Peter was very worried about Odette, who was captured with him in the south of France while on a mission to the Resistance movement. As long as they were both in Fresnes prison near Paris they had occasionally been able to pass messages but, after Peter's departure for Germany, they had of course completely lost touch. He had desperately hoped that she would turn up as a hostage, but she never did, although it had always been agreed that if caught they would pretend to be man and wife, so affording to Odette whatever protection the name Churchill might be worth. It had saved Peter and we still hoped it would have saved her.

The next day again dawned bright and clear and the car from Caserta called for us punctually. Once again we drove along the road to Allied Headquarters but this time, shortly before reaching the palace, we turned off through the trees to the right and came out on to an airstrip. After a short wait in Air Control, which passed pleasantly with a cup of tea and a chat with the crew, the Air Marshal arrived and we all went on board.

This was no stark troop-carrying aircraft but a Dakota most plushly fitted out for the transport of very senior officers. After recommending us to his steward, our host settled down to work at a table. Peter and I relaxed in our armchairs and watched first the Mediterranean and then France rolling back beneath us. Once again the captain and co-pilot were most agreeable, one or the other frequently coming aft to identify for us the cities and rivers over which we passed.

My most vivid memory of that journey was, however, the steward. I think someone must have told him that we had been starved for a couple of years for with the greatest regularity he came every half hour with sandwiches he had concocted for our delight. Starting with corned beef to take the edge off our appetites, he worked relentlessly through his repertoire, from sardines to pâté de foie, until both of us were replete. It was fortunate that the journey lasted no longer than it did.

We landed in the afternoon at Blackbushe and, as I could remember the telephone number of SOE in Baker Street, I sat down at the Station Commander's desk to report our arrival. At first I drew an absolute blank. My own Section had ceased to exist when the war in North Africa was over and nobody who had been connected with it seemed to be around. It was also Saturday afternoon and the war was over.

Then, tentatively, the girl on the switchboard asked if I was Squadron Leader Falconer. After two and a half years and believing me to be dead she had still recognised my voice. She put me through to the RAF Section which had administered me and from then on all was well. Wing Commander Redding and Vera Atkins, both of whom I knew well, were together in the office and, promising to tell Peter's people of his return, they said they would send a car.

The turnout which arrived was typical of SOE. The Air Marshal had gone off in a very ordinary staff car. What came for us was an enormous black Packard limousine with a FANY driver who looked as if she had stepped straight out of the pages of a wartime number of the *Tatler*. This magnificent equipage drew up outside the station building, viewed with awe by one and all. The vision behind the wheel stepped briskly out, whipped open the rear door and saluted smartly. Then she looked at us and burst into tears. The military tableau was spoiled, but a more moving welcome home it would have been difficult to imagine.

When we got to Baker Street, Peter dropped off at his Section where the first thing he was told was that Odette had come home that same day. From France she had been sent to Ravensbrück concentration camp for women, between Berlin and Stettin, and in the last days of the war had persuaded the Kommandant to bring her to the British lines. The name Churchill was again the vital factor.

I went on to the RAF Section to a welcome worth coming home to. Within a very short time I had a priority call through to my mother who, poor lady, must have had a considerable shock. The last she had heard of me had been two years before when I was reported as missing. My wife and daughter, I learned, were back in Cheltenham, having been brought to England the previous Autumn by the RAF. But when I rang they were out.

It was too late for me to get down to Gloucestershire that night but it was arranged that I should spend the night with Vera Atkins and her mother and ring my wife during the evening from their flat. A little later, my luggage augmented by a bottle of gin, a bottle of sherry and a sub-stantial wad of clothing coupons, Vera and I were on our way. Driving through London seemed very strange, until I realised that there was no more blackout.

That evening when I tried to make the call to Cheltenham the girl at the exchange said the lines were so congested that there was not a hope of getting through. Then Vera took over and gave her a graphic description of the circumstances. We were through within five minutes.

I cannot possibly describe the conversation which followed. My wife had no idea where I had been, or how I had been captured, or under what circumstances, or that I had been in concentration camps.

I had had no news of her or of our daughter since October 1942 – and we had three minutes. I suppose the only concrete information given was that I would be in Cheltenham next day on the London train at such and such a time.

The following morning Vera drove me to Paddington and a short time later I started once more on the journey I knew so well. The train was not particularly full and I had a carriage to myself. This was just as well for I was still dressed in my old trousers and my battledress top and I had no hat. I was also in no mood for conversation.

The train was by no means as fast as the pre-war 'Cheltenham Flyer' and we stopped more often. But every familiar station brought me nearer home and I loved them all. Reading, Didcot and Swindon, then Kemble and the beginning of the Cotswold country I knew so well, the Sapperton tunnel and down the Stroud valley through Brimscombe, Stroud, and Stonehouse and across the plain to Gloucester. There, as in the old days, we went into reverse and trundled gently through Churchdown to Cheltenham.

The impossible had happened and, in spite of the Gestapo, in spite of the concentration camps and in spite of Bader's orders to kill us all, I was home and safe.

My wife and daughter were waiting for me on the platform.

My wife was little changed in spite of four and a half years in occupied France where the food situation had been very much worse than it was in England.

My daughter, on the other hand, who had been not two years old when I had last seen her, was now a big girl of nearly seven. She looked wide-eyed at the father she had not seen for so long, but had never been allowed to forget.

My mother, who had a Victorian horror of showing emotion in public, was waiting outside in her car.

As far as I was concerned, after several days of American hospitality my appearance, apart from my deplorable clothes, while it shocked my wife was not nearly as repulsive as it had been even a week earlier.

Since her return from France my wife had been helping one of the House Ladies at Cheltenham Ladies' College, where my daughter was in Junior College, and improving the girls' French at the same time. However, as soon as they knew I was back the College authorities released her on the spot. She and our daughter joined my mother in her house outside Cheltenham.

We naturally had a good deal to talk about. When my wife and our daughter came back to England it was to find that there had been no news of me at all since I was reported missing early in 1943. If I had been in a PoW camp my mother would have had news of it but there had been none. Even so my wife steadfastly refused to believe that I would not return, clinging to the fact that SOE had only reported me as 'missing'. Shortly before my return they had started paying her an allowance 'as an interim measure'. In fact, they were just being tactful pending confirmation of my death and this was indeed a widow's pension.

I had to pay it back.

Little remains to be told. People knew where I had been and what my wife and daughter had been through and were very kind. The outfitters would not accept our clothing coupons and petrol seemed no problem. My tailor forgot about his waiting list and made me a new uniform in three days.

One of the most warming incidents occurred when I went back to London. I took my poor watch along to the people from whom I had bought it – Hughes of Fenchurch Street – to see if they could repair it.

The man in the shop told me, before even opening it, that there was a waiting list of at least ten months to a year.

When he saw the state of the machinery he looked at me severely and said he did not think they would be prepared to undertake it at all. He added that it was a pity that amateurs would insist in carrying out their repairs themselves. Protesting that, as an engineer myself, I knew my own limitations and would not dream of doing such a thing, I told him in detail what had actually happened – how the Gestapo interrogator in Tunis had deliberately opened the watch and used a pair of pliers to stir its machinery while pretending to be checking whether it was a compass or a map ... .

'Well,' he said, 'in that case come back in three days' time and we will see what we can do.'

When I went back three days later my watch was repaired and I was using it still thirty years later. They refused to accept any payment at all.

Epilogue

Lead us from hence, where we may leisurely
Each one demand an answer to his part
Perform'd in this wide gap of time since first
We were dissever'd.
***The Winter's Tale* Act V, Scene 3**

L ooking back on my adventures there can be no doubt at all that I was very lucky indeed. Had I been caught before the tide started to turn for the Germans, there would have been no question of gathering hostages and, had my dossier not been lost between Tunis and Berlin, I would not have been chosen as a hostage anyway.

I was fortunate that when I am engrossed in something it takes up the whole of my thoughts so that, at the critical times, I was able to push fear into the background.

I was luckier than the millions who died long, lingering and cruel deaths in the camps I was in and in all the many other camps.

And I was luckier than thousands of survivors because, as the Gestapo destroyed all records, they were never reunited with their families and never knew whether their husbands, their wives or their children were still alive or not.

I was lucky, having been captured under conditions for which the rules of war offer no protection, to have survived when millions who had committed no other crime than to be born of a race the Nazis were determined to exterminate, died under conditions it is difficult to imagine and will, I most earnestly pray, never be repeated.

What happened next?
I was asked to stay on in Germany after the war with the Military Government of BAOR (British Army of the Rhine) and invited to appear before a selection board, at which the conversation went something like this:

'What did you do during the war?'

'I was a saboteur.'

'Oh! What did you do before the war?'

'I was a professional engineer in the cement industry.'

This, I thought, would give them the clue for I knew that Military Government was taking over the control of manufacture of all strategic materials – which includes cement. However:

'In that case we have the very job for you. The Passport Control Services was run by the Gestapo under Nazi laws, which have been abrogated. It has to be re-organised from the word go. Will you take it on?'

'Yes.'

So, until I handed it over to the Federal Ministry of Internal Affairs in 1951, that is what I did. In one way only was my past experience of value – I knew a Nazi when I saw one and was able to keep them out of my organisation. This task completed, I went back to the cement industry.

There are people who, having read about the adventures of a group of people, like to know what happened to them afterwards. To trace the subsequent lives of 136 men, women and children would be a very difficult task but here is what I know of some of my fellow hostages.

BLUM, Léon (1872–1950)
In 1946 he again formed a socialist government in France and was the last Prime Minister before the creation of the Fourth Republic.

CHURCHILL, Peter, Captain (1909–1972)
Shortly after the war, Peter and Odette were married and I visited them several times in their house on Notting Hill. The marriage, however, was

not a success and they were divorced in, as far as I remember, the early 1950s. Peter returned to his favourite part of the world – the south of France.

DAY, H.M.A, 'Wings', Wing Commander (1898–1977)
He returned to the RAF, finally retired and lived in Kent. We last met in 1970.

DELBOS, Yvon (1885–1956)
He returned to France to his flat in the Ile Saint Louis in Paris and dived back into political life. As a bachelor his essential privacy was savagely guarded by his housekeeper and, the first time I rang up, I was told firmly that the Minister was not at home, but would I care to leave my name and telephone number? This was no good to me as I was only in Paris for the day so I asked her to tell Monsieur le Ministre that it was the editor of the *Echo d'Oranienburg* speaking.

A few seconds later Yvon himself was on the line begging us to come round without delay. We had a most enjoyable reunion and he told me about his meeting at a diplomatic cocktail party with Molotov.

Yvon at once asked after his nephew Kokorin, to which Molotov replied that he had no nephew. Yvon explained that he really meant his wife's nephew, Vassili Vassiliev Kokorin, who had been a prisoner in Germany. Molotov replied icily that there had been no Russian prisoners in Germany, and that was that. And that was why Kokorin joined the Yugoslav partisans rather than return to his own country.

Yvon held various high offices in the French Government from 1947 to 1950.

Freiherr von FALKENHAUSEN, Alexander, General (1878–1966)
He had been military governor of Brussels during the German occupation of Belgium so was handed over to the Belgians as a war criminal. I had never been able to suppose that this great gentleman could have done anything to merit such an accusation, and criticism of him by one of our SS guards bore this out.

Also, when I was in Germany after the war and his trial was pending, I mentioned his name to a member of the Belgian Military

Mission. This officer, who had been in Belgium throughout the occupation, said that Falkenhausen's administration of the city had played a vital part in saving it from a reign of terror. He went so far as to say that, if ever the Belgians were to erect a statue to commemorate the man who had best served Belgium during the war, it should be of Falkenhausen.

There was in fact a strong body of opinion in favour of the general's acquittal but at that time there were political involvements which complicated the issue, particularly between Church and State. Falkenhausen, who could have called on powerful support from ecclesiastical witnesses, refused to subpoena them for fear of damaging the Church's cause. He declared that he would rely entirely on volunteers and it appears that political considerations outweighed the love of justice, for very few witnesses offered themselves on his behalf.

He was found guilty and sentenced to a term of imprisonment which was more or less accounted for by the time he had already been in confinement awaiting trial. He had, nevertheless many loyal friends in the country who saw to it that he did not lack comforts and the lady who organised this was later to become his wife.

I was still in charge of Passport Control in Germany when Falkenhausen was released and I had great pleasure in going down to Aachen to welcome him home.

McGRATH, John, Lieutenant Colonel (1893-1946)

He returned to Dublin but died not very long afterwards. He had been captured in 1940 whilst serving with the British Expeditionary Force. Perhaps trying to mislead the Germans over the Irish Brigade told on his health more than he was prepared to admit.

MÜLLER, Josef 'Ochsensepp', Doktor (1898–1979)

He became Minister of Justice of Bavaria after being instrumental in founding the Bavarian political party the CSU (*Christliche-Soziale Union*), later combined with its coalition partner the CDU (*Christliche Demokratische Union*).

I last met Müller in Munich in 1960 when we visited Dachau together and it was after this visit that a curious thing happened. I had taken a whole film of colour transparencies of the camp – of the cells we had occupied, of the torture chamber, of the crematorium and so on. When I sent this film to AGFA in Germany to be developed it was returned to me with a letter of apology because (they said) it had been damaged while being developed. They enclosed the only exposure which had survived this sabotage, a picture of the monument erected after the war to those who had died in the camp. This is the only time a film of mine has ever been 'damaged while being developed'.

In 1975 Ochsensepp published his memoirs, *Bis zur letzten Konsequenz*. This is a very valuable contribution to the history of resistance within Germany to the Nazi régime from its inception to its final collapse.

NIEMOELLER, Martin, Pastor (1892–1984)

He became a very prominent leader of the Protestant Church in Germany and when we met (which we did several times) he always greeted me with the greatest affection. However, as his interpretation of doctrine became more and more peculiar, we tended to lose touch.

He also suffered, like a great many other reverend gentlemen at the present time, from an urge to dabble in politics. For this he was very ill equipped, sadly lacking in worldly wisdom and tending to ascribe to people and governments of declared atheist outlook the goodwill towards men which is propounded in the Gospels, and presuming a sincerity on the part of those governments which he himself possessed but which has no part in the power politics of today.

In 1951 I was handing over my Passport Control Service (*Bundespasskontrolldienst*) to the German Federal Government but had some trouble in persuading the Minister concerned in accepting it as it stood (which the Allied High Commission were anxious should be the case). Niemoeller made so inflammatory a speech on some political issue, implying that the minister (who was a Niemoeller fan) shared his view, that the Minister was forced to resign and I had to start all over again with his successor.

I last heard from Martin in 1971.

PAPAGOS, Alexandro, General (1883–1955)

He returned to Greece to command the Greek forces against the Communist insurgents then went into politics. He was Prime Minister from 1952 and died in office on 4 October 1955.

PIGUET, Gabriel, Monseigneur (1887–1952)

Bishop of Clermont in France, he returned from Naples to a most moving and triumphant welcome from the people of his diocese. In an interview with Radio Auvergne he said:

> I have come back from very far away and I speak, not of kilometres, but of the dangers and sufferings I have been through with dear friends of whom, alas, too many less fortunate than I will never return. It is of them that I think and for them that I pray in this moment of joy on coming back to my beloved Auvergne.

Monseigneur Piguet died shortly after he had completed his book about his experiences *Prison et Déportation*.

SCHACHT, Hjalmar (1877–1970)

He succeeded in getting himself acquitted at the Nuremberg trial, although it was his financial genius which had enabled Hitler to stabilise the German Mark. It is my belief that, as President of the Reichsbank, he arranged for himself to be arrested in order to be on the right side of the fence when Germany should eventually collapse.

After Nuremberg it remained for him to be 'de-nazified' by a German court. He started proceedings in his home town of Tingleff in Schleswig Holstein but, realising that he was not going to get away with it, he managed to have the case transferred to the Lüneburge Heide. This area had always been strongly pro-Nazi because of the very considerable concessions in tax relief and exemption from conscription granted to the farming community by the Hitler régime and for which Schacht himself was largely responsible.

He was given a clean sheet and subsequently made a great name for himself sorting out the economic problems of emerging nations.

It seems odd that the man who had made Hitler's Germany financially possible should have been able after the war to capitalise on his experience.

von SCHUSCHNIGG, Kurt, Chancellor of Austria (1897–1977)

He was Chancellor from 1934 to 1938. He took no further part in politics after the war and emigrated to the United States with his wife Vera (née Countess Czernin) and daughter Maria-Dolores who was born in a concentration camp. He was naturalised an American citizen in 1956.

STETSKO, Yaroslav (1912–1986)

We have met him and his wife Slava again on many occasions. He was the leading light and President of the Anti-Bolshevic Bloc of Nations (ABN) which had its headquarters in Munich. He travelled all over the world addressing anti-Bolshevic organisations on the evils of Communism. He had a very wide following in many countries in every continent but at the time it was difficult to see what could be achieved.

This very frail man survived my father but sadly did not live to see the fall of the Berlin Wall in 1989 or the collapse of the USSR. ECS

Of the three princes, Friedrich Leopold of Prussia, Philipp of Hesse and Xavier of Bourbon, I have been able to find out nothing at all. Bishop Piguet tells how he travelled with Xavier from Paris south by train after their release and that Xavier's family was waiting to greet him on the platform at Moulins.

And finally, what of the two non-hostage Germans with whom I was most concerned – Kaindl of Sachsenhausen and Captain von Alvensleben?

KAINDL, Anton, SS Standartenführer (1902–1948)

Shortly after the end of the war a skinny civilian with impeccable papers passed through a Field Security checkpoint. So impeccable, however, were his papers that the sergeant, his suspicions aroused, called him back by the name on the papers. When this produced no reaction he arrested the civilian.

He was thought to be Kaindl of Sachsenhausen but this, of course, he hotly denied. I was therefore asked to go down from Detmold where I was stationed at the time to Paderborn to have a look at him.

It was Kaindl all right but he went on denying it. When I asked him if he was calling me a liar, he said yes. I therefore had the pleasure of belting him over the ear on behalf of several hundred thousand prisoners who had suffered at his hands. Supposing no doubt that, as was the habit of the Gestapo of which he had been an ornament, this was only the beginning of a masterly beating up (in which, of course, he was quite wrong) he at once broke down, started snivelling, and admitted that he was indeed the ex-Kommandant of Sachsenhausen.

We listened patiently to the usual spiel that he was only carrying out orders from above, that he had only joined the Nazi Party to keep his job and save his wife and family from starving, that he had never approved of the methods of the Gestapo and had, at great risk to his life, managed to avoid carrying out the more brutal of the directives he received, and so on ad nauseam.

Because so many Russians had suffered at his hands and because Sachsenhausen was in the Russian Zone of Germany, he was handed over to the Soviet authorities for trial. Some years later I heard from a refugee from East Germany that Kaindl was employed doing what he did best – running a concentration camp for the Russians.

ALVENSLEBEN, Freiherr Wichard von, Captain

At the beginning of 1947 when life was hard for the average German citizen, a man came asking for me at my house in Bünde, Westphalia, where I was stationed at the time. This turned out to be von Alvensleben, sometime captain in the Wehrmacht, and the man who had rescued us from the Gestapo in Villabassa.

The British were cutting down thousands of trees in the Harz mountain for pit props and Alvensleben, desperately trying to scratch a living when the Reichsmark was almost valueless and the only way to get food was to have something to barter for it, had obtained permission to excavate the tree roots and sell them as firewood.

The only way to recover this timber at an economic rate was to use explosives, but for this he needed a permit from the Military Government which he was having the greatest difficulty in obtaining. Would I be prepared to help?

I was, of course, delighted to vouch for his integrity, which was all that was really needed, and I believe his business prospered.

Glossary of Comparable Military Ranks
(mentioned in the book)

Waffen–SS is the normal abbreviation of Waffen–Schutzstaffel or Armed Protection Squad (The Nazi State Praetorian Guard)

SS Rank	Translation of SS Rank	Wehrmacht Rank	British Rank
Commissioned Officer Grades			
Reichsführer	Empire Leader of the SS	None	None
Obergruppenführer	Senior Group Leader	General der Infanterie etc.	Lieutenant General
Standartenführer	Standard Leader	Oberst	Colonel
Obersturmbannführer	Senior Storm Command Leader	Oberstleutnant	Lieutenant Colonel
Obersturmführer	Senior Storm Leader	Oberleutnant	Lieutenant
Untersturmführer	Under Storm Leader	Leutnant	Second Lieutenant
Non Commissioned Officer Grades			
Oberscharführer	Senior Company Leader	Feldwebel	Company Sergeant Major
Unterscharführer	Under Company Leader	Unteroffizier	Sergeant

Feldgendarmerie
They were the uniformed military police units of the armies of the German Empire (including the Wehrmacht) from 1810 in Saxony until the conclusion of the Second World War.

Appendix 1

Bibliography

This book has been written from memory and after several decades there may well be errors. If so, these are of detail only. Experiences of this sort are not lightly forgotten. In this connection it may well be maintained that, after so long a time, the conversations I have recorded in direct speech cannot possibly be word perfect. This is, with a few exceptions, true.

I have, however, preferred to use this method of reporting because I find it the easiest, and indeed the least tedious, way of establishing the tone of these exchanges particularly when for reasons I hope will be clear I was trying to be either provocative or just downright offensive.

Where possible I have checked dates and names and I owe thanks to the authors of the books I have used for this purpose. They are:

Bosanquet, Mary, *The Life and Death of Dietrich Bonhöffer* (Hodder & Stoughton, London, 1968)

Bryant, Arthur, *The Turn of the Tide* (Doubleday, London, 1957)

Delarue, Jacques, *The History of the Gestapo* (Transworld, London, 1962)

Müller, Josef, *Bis zur letzten Konsequenz* (Süddeutscher Verlag, Munich, 1975)

Piguet, Gabriel, *Prison et Déportation* (Éditions Spes, Paris, 1947; reprinted L'echelle de Jacob, Paris, 2009)

Vermehren, Isa, *Reise durch den letzten Akt. Ravensbrück, Buchenwald, Dachau: eine Frau berichtet* (Christian Wegner Verlag, Hamburg, 1946)

Appendix 2

Note by Evelyn Campbell Smith (née Falconer)

M any people as well as my father have wondered how Germans could have sunk to the depths of depravity and cruelty flaunted during the Second World War and before. In this appendix are sections moved from various chapters of the book in which my father voiced his speculations and used quotations from some of the books in the bibliography listed in Appendix 1. The sections were moved because they held up the narrative but are important in their own right.

Please also read the extracts from Keyserling's *Das Spektrum Europas* which I have added as it may help to understand how Germany disgraced itself in the way it did from 1933 to 1945.

Hugh Mallory Falconer

It may seem from this book that, in my opinion, all Germans are stupid. If this were indeed the case it would be a sad reflection that it took the combined might of the British Empire, the United States of America and Russia until 1945 to achieve victory. Such men as Raeder, Kesselring and Rommel were highly skilled and competent professionals. Had they and others like them not been subordinate to the whims of an amateur guided by impulse, instinct and the stars, who shall say what the outcome might have been? The Allies might well have had to start the defeat of Nazism by the liberation of Britain.

I do indeed refer in this book to men who, of my own knowledge, were very gallant gentlemen: men such as Ochsensepp Müller and Dietrich Bonhöffer and General Alexander von Falkenhausen who, in the last days of our captivity, was the saviour of us all.

Nor are the leaders of the abortive coup of the 20th July 1944 to be forgotten: men such as Karl Friedrich Görderler and Claus Count Schenck von Stauffenberg who, in their attempt to bring Hitler down, paid the penalty of an ignominious death.

From Chapter 3

It was only later that I was to meet men like Josef Müller and Dietrich Bonhöffer who, from the time war broke out, worked continuously and steadfastly to bring down the Nazi régime. They did this, not with the intermittent bravery of soldiers in action, but with the cold courage which faces death day by day, hour by hour, month by month and year after year – the cruelty, humiliation and savage death which caught up with such men as Admiral Canaris in the last days of the war and which Müller escaped by a miracle.

From Chapter 7

There are to this day many thousands of numbered accounts in Swiss banks on which no operation has taken place for decades and, while many of them were opened by Jews and others who died in concentration camps, some at least belonged to high Nazi officials who never lived to enjoy them. Others were no doubt enjoyed to the full.

From Chapter 9

Quotations from the four books mentioned:

1) Doctor Josef Müller, German lawyer and Minister of Justice
   Bis zur letzten Konsequenz – Süddeutscher Verlag, Munich, 1975

Of Flossenbürg he wrote:

> We were taken to the cell block and locked up in cells which, I later discovered, had been made available just before our arrival by the simple method of liquidating their previous tenants ....
>
> Orders were given that I should not only be handcuffed but also fitted with leg irons – with steel rings about three centimetres broad; these fetters were so tightly locked on to my ankles that it was impossible to move at all ....
>
> At the interrogation on the following day the Gestapo officer had obviously already decided that he would see me hang. He began by hitting me on the mouth with all his strength; shrieking 'I'll make you talk, you swine' he repeatedly struck me with his fist ....

On another day I saw prisoners – grown-ups and children – driven out of showers on to the road which ran through the camp. There they were made to stand, stark naked, in the bitter cold which followed the sunset, until they froze to death.

2) Isa Vermehren, German singer *Reise durch den letzten Akt* – Wegner Verlag, Hamburg, 1947

One evening, at about half past nine, we heard the wardress unlock the cell door of a Polish pianist – we only knew her as 'Mimi' – and tell her to come at once. 'You can leave your things here,' she added. A quarter of an hour later we heard steps and hushed voices behind the compound wall, and then the sound of a shot. Then there was a terrified scream – another shot – and silence. Then again: steps, a shot, silence ... steps, a shot, silence.

Next day there was a nauseous black smoke from the crematorium; the Pole and seven women from the camp had been shot. The same thing happened a few days later and we counted twenty-one shots: twenty-one Polish women had been liquidated. In this way died Helena, a young German girl, English by marriage, who had landed in Germany with her husband by parachute as a secret agent. Denounced shortly afterwards, she had been held in a dark cell for two years until the Kommandant came to tell her that she was to receive better treatment. Two days later she was taken from her cell and one more shot rang out behind the wall.

3) Monseigneur Gabriel Piguet, Bishop of Clermont, Frenchman *Prison et Déportation* – Éditions Spes, Paris, 1947

Of Natzweiler he wrote:

My cassock, my pectoral cross and my episcopal ring quickly brought me to the attention of the brutal guards. Without intermission I was so grossly insulted that French fellow prisoners who understood German refused to translate such obscenities.

Now we were called out in alphabetical order. There in the open we were relieved of our luggage, of whatever food we had with us, of all our personal possessions, and stripped to the skin. My pectoral cross and episcopal ring were taken away.

In Natzweiler, as in every other concentration camp, all religious books and objects were forbidden. As a guard said 'Here, there is no God!' When General Delestraint complained of the treatment meted out to him as a French Corps Commander, the SS reply was 'Here, there are no generals. Here, you are a number. Here, you come in through the gate and you leave through the crematorium.'

The inhuman shouts of the guards, the enormous dogs trained to attack the prisoners, the unmentionable atrocities, the separation from everything including the most personal and essential things, made me realise that I was plunged into the most miserable conditions possible for a human being to suffer.

4) Michael Hollard, Frenchman Resistance worker *The man who saved London: the story of Michel Hollard, DSO, Croix de Guerre –* Martelli, George (1961) – Odhams Press.

Of the transport of prisoners to Germany and of Neuengamme concentration camp Michel Hollard, a Frenchman who had worked as a British agent, wrote:

The second day passed like the first, except that the prisoners were weaker. Tortured by thirst, panting for air, some collapsed while others became feverish. Once or twice a day, during the stop at some station, a bottle of water was passed surreptitiously by some good Samaritan in defiance of the guards. One prisoner fell ill from drinking his own urine and became delirious. At the next stop an appeal was made to the guards to remove him but, like all such requests, it was simply ignored. Sometime during the night the man's cries ceased. In the morning he was found to be dead.

This treatment was quite deliberate and, from a Nazi point of view, entirely logical. Deportation had a double objective: to remove enemies of the Reich and to obtain slave labour. Hitler's Germany had no use for weaklings and one of the purposes of the journey was to kill them off. Those strong enough to survive it would also be good, it was calculated, for at least several months in a labour camp.

In February 1945 a number of boys between nine and fourteen, who had only recently arrived, were seen to enter the block used as an infirmary. None of them left it alive. It was afterwards learnt that they had all been lethally inoculated after being submitted to a series of biological experiments. Three French doctors who refused to take part in the experiments were executed in turn for trying to prevent them ... .

At Fresnes and the other German prisons in France and even in the transit camp of Royal-Lieu-Compiègne the guards had been soldiers of the Wehrmacht. Consisting mostly of older men called up for the war, they were civilians in uniform with normal human feelings.

But the SS were a different race, almost a different species, educated and conditioned for one purpose: to assure the supremacy of the Nazi State. In the process they had been dehumanised and were no longer men but monsters: brutish, violent and pitiless. Even among themselves they never laughed or even smiled; their faces were masks set permanently in an expression which combined stubborn stupidity with callous indifference.

From Chapter 12

In case I be accused of anti-German bias in my criticism of the Sippenhäftlinge and the German petite noblesse, I would like to quote again from the book by Isa Vermehren:

Reise durch den letzten Akt – Wegner Verlag, Hamburg, 1947

One evening we received twenty loaves, a pot of jam, two pounds of butter, two sausages, two packets of tobacco, two cartons of cigarettes, a huge bag of biscuits and another of sweets.

But the general delight engendered by this gift degenerated into the greedy fear that one's neighbour's share might be greater than one's own and particularly that the person charged with the apportioning could be setting aside too great a part as compensation for his labours. This nightly revictualling was carefully kept secret from the occupants of the other room – ostensibly for fear that it might in that way be discovered by the SS, but in fact to avoid the painful duty of having to share.

The more we received, the greater was the bitterness with which each person strove to ensure that he received his just part and, if possible, more.

From Chapter 15

The Americans, our Allies, were actually here. We were no longer being guarded by Germans against Germans. The moment of release about which I had so often dreamt had come at last and it is difficult to describe my feelings.

Of course from the moment the US Army turned up a great many things happened very fast.

Also, I think that an all wise Providence takes care that the human mind is not taxed beyond its limits, either with sudden joy or sudden despair. There were facts that I suddenly realised at intervals throughout the day, but not all at once, for that I believe could have been intolerable.

There was the realisation that now I would see my family again after all, although this was tempered by the fact that I had had no news of them since January 1943.

There was the realisation that the shadow of death was at last entirely gone and needed no more thrusting into the background of my mind.

Still later there was the realisation that I would, after all, be able to do the things I wanted to do, and see the places I wanted to see and that, at least at the hands of the Gestapo, I was not to die young.

And all these thoughts gradually built up to a crescendo of joyful exultation. But then I thought of the friends I had made while in captivity: of Graf von Halem and the Bishop of Lublin, of Michael Cumberlege and Raymond Amar, and above all of Dietrich Bonhöffer – and they were all dead. And thought that unadulterated happiness is beyond the hope of man.

Why, it may asked, again bring up all this business of Nazi brutality decades after the event? The Federal Republic of Germany is now an accepted democratic country, a rich and important member of the European Union, and altogether respectable.

The reason is that it could happen again – not just in Germany but almost anywhere. Indeed, it is a way of bringing about the subjection of a nation of which the Communists appeared to be aware.

If the economy of a country is depressed, if money is scarce and there are many people unemployed – in short, if hunger and misery are rife – then, sooner or later, something unpleasant is going to happen.

What happened in Germany was that at a time of despair and depression brought about by the intransigence of the Treaty of Versailles and the incompetence of the Weimar Republic, a group of ruthless and energetic men got together and preached a new philosophy. They built up their private army (the SA) and what was at first their private bodyguard (the SS), and started a campaign of terror which the police force was at first too apathetic to oppose and then too frightened to resist.

In 1933 Hitler's NSDAP (*Nationalsozialistische Deutsche Arbeiterpartei*) became the elected government and by 1934 the only legal party. The leaders, all opposition crushed and the Gestapo paramount, now put into practice the creed they had always preached.

Their target was national prosperity and strength, territorial expansion and the elimination of the Jews and they pressed on towards it with relentless zeal, without pity and without mercy. Among the hungry, the frustrated and the fanatical they found enough pitiless and merciless people to carry out their orders and promote their purpose, namely the cold-blooded elimination of all opposition, at first within Germany itself and then in other countries as they came under Nazi domination.

It is too easy to say 'It could only have happened in Germany'. It could have happened in any country suffering severely enough from poverty and depression. And it could happen again, given the same circumstances. Any nation, however civilised, could muster a nucleus of sadists such as the Nazis used. If the country's youth movement is properly organised, it only takes about eight years to corrupt a whole generation into perverted thugs – such as the men who committed the atrocity of Oradour-sur-Glane and the men and women who ran concentration camps like Ravensbrück and Auschwitz. And every year another contingent comes off the production line. The principles a man has learnt as a child are those which will govern his adult life.

There are neo-Nazi movements today which, underlining that Hitler brought Germany from misery to prosperity and world status, advocate his methods as the one remedy for the ills of our tottering world economy. But they do not talk of people living in terror, or parents put to death because their children betrayed them to the Secret Police, of industry made solvent by slave labour, of millions dying in concentration camps because they were thought to disagree with the Party in power.

One sees young people wearing the swastika as an ornament but they know nothing of the horrors of which it was the symbol or that they are displaying an object which, for more than twelve years, was the badge of oppression and terror.

Note by Evelyn Campbell Smith (née Falconer)
After my father's words come those I found in the book on Europe written by a twentieth century German philosopher, Count Hermann Keyserling.

He examined the individual characteristics of the peoples of Europe in a book published in 1928, so five years before Hitler came to power. He was a German Baltic nobleman. It is a remarkably prescient book written by a scholar who knew his own people extremely well!

Count Hermann Keyserling
Europe (Das Spektrum Europas) (1928)
Translated by Maurice Samuel
Published in Great Britain by Jonathan Cape
The following quotations from the chapter on Germany may help us all to understand how the people of Nazi Germany came to this pass.

Given a prevailing idea which conforms to reality and ... can be transposed into reality, the German people can achieve what no other people can ... It is the same, fundamentally, with every great German enterprise; its possibilities depend, time after time, on German self-sacrifice for the sake of the idea ... . German objectivity, therefore is the psychological root of specifically German idealism as well as of German spinelessness ... .

We have come now to the characteristic German feature ... and that is the unreality of the German spirit ... . It is typical of the German spirit that it lives for itself in a sphere of its own ... and the result is that fundamentally German knowledge is out of touch both with personal and with external reality ... . What he (the German) likes is to dictate ideals and programmes independently of the will of the participants. He demonstrates this in every official order ... this is implied by the dominance of stark formulation of ideas, whose logical content and logical sequence are regarded as of more importance than the living persons to whom they are applied.

As a type the German is a scholar... . The German scholar-spirit is all the more uncanny to other peoples because it finds its instrument in that lack of moderation which is traditionally German ... it is the one characteristic which foreign critics have always unanimously observed, and which the German himself only imperfectly sees as a function of his feeling for space, his longing for infinity ... if it once becomes 'practical' (it) can produce a high degree of mass-organisation. For in this wise the life of millions simply subjects itself to an idea. The rule of the idea becomes absolute; individual personality is simply wiped out of the picture.

The German **needs** external discipline as the balancing weight to his inner freedom ... . Because the same thing applies to the overwhelming majority of Germans, democracy in the English sense is of little use to them ... . England is free from envy, to the extent that every person really counts. Germany may play the democratic game to her heart's content; the fact remains that, in his inmost being, every German knows that as far as Germany is concerned everything depends upon the few ... this explains certain peculiar phenomena which hardly anyone understands ... instinctively the German dreams of a leader who, by virtue of his very standing, is lifted above all comparison; that leader, again, be he ever so German, is by his very position free from envy.

And what if that leader is an unworthy hero such as Hitler? As we follow Keyserling's chapter on the Germany of 1928 we can see how this type of nation could and did step by step transform a significant proportion of itself into the set of unfeeling monsters which the Nazis became.

End Notes

Chapter 2: SOE
1. Extract from *The Secret History of SOE*
2. Extract from *The Secret History of SOE*
3. Extract from *The Secret History of SOE*

Chapter 3: In Tunis Gaol
1. See Appendix 2

Chapter 7: The Hostages
1. See Appendix 2

Chapter 9: The Nazi Way
1. See Appendix 2

Chapter 12: The Road to Dachau
1. See Appendix 2.

Chapter 15: The Southern Redoubt
1. See Appendix 2.

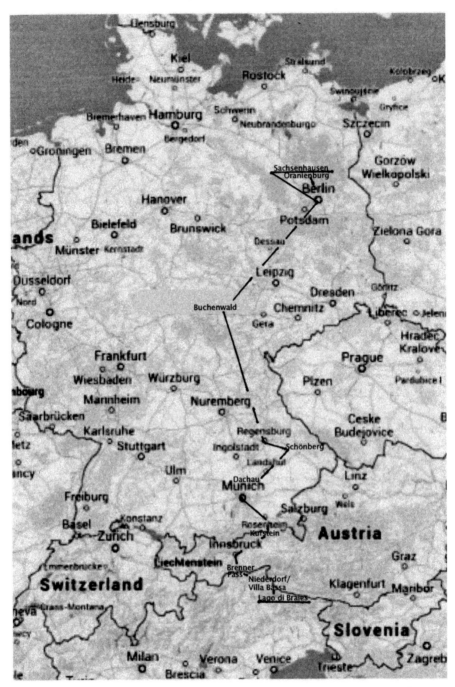

Map showing moves from Berlin to concentration camps to the
Southern Redoubt and Lago di Braies

Index

Alvensleben, Bodo von, Count, 98–9, 106, 112–13, 159

Alvensleben, Freiherr Wichard von, Capt., 159–62, 165, 186–7

Amar, Raymond, 69–72, 196

Ameche, Don, 169

Amici, 169

Anderson, Kenneth, Lt Gen., 8

Arnim von, Elizabeth, 21

Atkins, Vera, 176–7

Bader, 140, 142, 144, 146–50, 152–6, 158, 161, 177

Bairnsfather, Bruce, 74

Bandera, Stepan, 70

Bell, Dr Bishop of Chichester, 107

Bessonov, I G , Gen., 61, 78–9, 135, 167

Best, Sigismund Payne, Capt., 57, 61, 93, 106, 129

Bethge, Eberhardt 108

Blohm = Blum?, 172

Blum, Léon, 61, 69, 102, 137, 167, 172, 181

Blum, Madame, 61, 79, 102, 137, 140, 145

Bonhöffer, Dietrich, Pastor, 91, 104, 106–108, 114, 118, 122–5, 134, 167, 191–2, 196

Bosanquet, Mary, 108, 190

Bourbon, Xavier, Prince of, 61, 130–1, 145, 167, 186

Braun, Eva, 151

Bryant, Arthur, 190

Canaris, Wilhelm, Adm., 104, 107, 125, 134, 139, 192

Casement, Roger, Sir, 135

Churchill, Jack, Col., 61, 135, 149, 155

Churchill, Peter, Capt., 61, 78–9, 134–5, 139–40, 142, 149–150, 164–5, 171, 173–6, 181

Churchill, Winston, Prime Minister, 37, 74

Ciano, Gian Galeazzo, 8

Cukor, George, 170

Cumberlege, Michael, Cdr., 70, 93, 135, 196

Cushing, 169

Day, Harry, W/Cdr., 'Wings', 78, 93, 134–5, 138, 150, 158, 163, 166, 182

Delarue, Jacques, 190

Delbos, Yvon, 50, 52, 57, 70, 93, 182

Delestraint, Charles, Gen., 194

Delmer, Sefton, 168
Dowse, Sidney, 135

Eisenhower, Dwight, Gen., 151

Falkenhausen, Freiherr Alexander
    von, Gen., 70, 93, 98–9, 106, 116,
    116–17, 127, 140–1, 150–1, 156,
    158–9, 161, 166, 182–3, 191
Ferrero, Davido, Col., 130, 150,
    157, 169
Franco, Francisco, Gen., 5
Franz, the gardener, 44, 75–6
Fritz, Alsatian guard dog, 146–8

Garibaldi, Sante, Gen., 130, 150,
    152, 157–8, 160, 163, 169, 173
Gehre, Ludwig, 103, 106, 114,
    125, 134
Genghis Khan, 164
Gisevius, Anneliese, 120
Goebbels, Joseph, Dr, 45, 59–60, 74,
    77, 84, 138, 151
Gördeler, Karl Friedrich, 118, 191
Goering, Hermann Wilhelm, 58,
    60, 151
Goethe, Johann Wolfgang von, 65

Halder, Franz, Gen., 70, 151
Halem, Count/Graf von,
    53, 69–72, 196
Hattrell, Mr, of Horley, 172
Heberlein, Erich, Dr, 93, 98, 119, 123
Heberlein, Margot, Frau, 93, 98–9,

106, 116, 122–4
Heidi, prostitute, 113, 116, 119,
    122–3, 132, 138, 167, 172
Hesse, Philip, Prince of, 61, 137,
    144–5, 186
Himmler, Heinrich, Reichsführer,
    vii, 60–1, 88, 104
Hitler, Adolf, Chancellor, 5, 44,
    59–60, 62, 71, 84–5, 92, 104,
    118–120, 134–5, 139, 151, 185–6,
    191, 196–8, 200
Hollard, Michael, 90, 194
Horthy junior, Nikolaus, 167
Hughes of Fenchurch
    Street, 23, 178

Ikarius, Sturmscharführer, 54, 56,
    64–5, 86, 92–3, 110

James 'Jimmy', 135
Jehovah's Witnesses, 44

Kaindl, Anton, Kommandant
    Sachsenhausen, 61, 64–5, 78, 87,
    92, 95, 143, 186–7
Kallay, Nikolaus von, 167
Kaltenbrünner, Ernst, 75
Karl the barber, 44–5, 48, 51, 71,
    91–2, 139, 173
Kesselring, Albert, FM, 191
Keyserling, Hermann, Count, 191,
    198, 200
Koch, Karl Otto, Kommandant
    Buchenwald, 61, 108–10

Koch, Ilse, Frau, 108–110
Kokorin, Vassili Vassiliev, 53, 56–7,
    61, 69, 72, 93, 106, 122, 125,
    135, 167, 182
Kohlenklau, 137–8
Kramer, Josef, Kommandant
    Auschwitz, 61

Leibholz, Gerhard, Oxford
    Lecturer, 125
Leibholz, Sabine, née Bonhöffer, 125
Liedig, Franz, Col., 139, 150
Lublin, Bishop of, 54, 70, 130, 196
Luther, Martin, 48
Lux, Unterscharführer, 54, 81,
    83, 93, 120

'Mallory', S/Ldr, 8–9
Mafalda, Princess of Savoy, 137,
    144–5
Max, 12–14, 17–19, 22–4, 27–8,
    30, 33, 66
McGrath John, Col., 135–7, 140,
    155–6, 183
Meyer, Unterscharführer,
    54–6, 120
Model, Walter, FM, 151
Molotov, Vyacheslav Mikhailovich,
    53, 56, 182
Montgomery of Alamein, Bernard
    Law, Viscount 8, 58, 151
Müller, Josef, Dr 'Ochsensepp',
    90–1, 103–4, 106, 114, 130, 134,
    150, 172, 183–4, 190–2

Mussolini, Benito, *Il Duce*, 8

Neuhauesler, Johannes, Msgr, 130, 134
Niemoeller, Martin, Pastor, 61, 130,
    134, 163–5, 184

Odette, 79, 135, 174–6, 181

Papagos, Alexander, FM, 78, 135,
    156, 185
Paulus, Friedrich, FM, 58
Piguet, Gabriel, Msgr, Bishop of
    Clermont, 90, 130–1, 134, 185–6,
    190, 193
Prussia, Friedrich Leopold,
    Prince of, 145, 186
Puender, Hermann, 106

Rabenau, Friedrich von, Gen., 98–9,
    107, 117–18, 125
Raeder, Erich, Adm., 151, 191
Rascher, Sigmund, Dr, 88–9, 106,
    109–11, 114, 119, 122, 126–9,
    131–2
Redding, W/Cdr., SOE, 176
Rommel, Erwin, FM, 58, 191

Schacht, Hjalmar, Dr, 70, 166, 168,
    172, 185
Schaeffer, Willi, cabaret artist, 138
Schiller, Friedrich von, 65
Schlabrendorff, Fabian von, Freiherr,
    139, 150
Schmidt, Unterscharführer, 54–7,

61, 68–70, 72–3, 77–8, 86, 91–2,
103, 120
Schmidz, Richard, Dr, 145
Schuschnigg, Kurt von, Chancellor
of Austria, 61, 145, 167, 186
Schuschnigg, Maria-Dolores, 145,
162, 186
Schuschnigg, Vera, Frau von, 79,
145, 186
Shakespeare, William, 65
Stalin's son, 61
Stauffenberg, Claus Schenck von,
Graf, 118, 172, 191
Stetzko, Yaroslav, 52–3, 70, 72,
75, 186
Stetzko, Slava, 186
Stevens, Richard, Major, later Lt
Col., 61, 129

Stiller, Escort Commander, 113–7,
122–3, 125–7, 132, 140, 142–4,
148–150, 152–6

Thyssen, Anneliese, Frau, 145
Thyssen, Fritz, 145, 166
Todt, Fritz, 61

Vansittart, Lord, vii
Vermehren, Isa, 90, 190, 193, 195
Victor Emmanuel, King of Italy, 131
Victoria, Queen, 139

Walsh, (Irishman), 169
Wymeersch, van, Belgian pilot,
138, 167